FROM HARDSHIPS TO STEAMSHIPS

from Hardships *to* Steamships

Memoirs of a Merchant Seaman during World War II

Charlie Workman

UNITED WRITERS
Cornwall

UNITED WRITERS PUBLICATIONS LTD
Ailsa, Castle Gate, Penzance, Cornwall.

British Library Cataloguing in Publication Data:
A catalogue record for this book is
available from the British Library.

ISBN 1 85200 108 9

Printed in Great Britain by
United Writers Publications Ltd
Cornwall.

Dedication

There are quite a few people to thank for this book and it is only fair to say and mention them all.

First is my cousin Joyce Cooper, now sadly deceased, who originally begged me to try and get my memories onto paper. Then another cousin Alan Workman who word processed all my handwritten scrawl. Alan had for a long time sung opera with the Sadler's Wells Opera Company, until retirement, and helped me immensely.

My dear wife Edna, who suffered my silences; Heather and Janice, my two patient daughters. And Jim, my younger brother, whose advice was so valued in matters Naval. I must also mention my granddaughter Victoria, for her photocopying skills and IT advice.

Finally, a dedication to the thousands of decent lads who lost their lives in the Merchant Service and those seamen who have crossed the bar since then.

Contents

1

Our Arrival in Hindpool

Our little procession moved slowly along the streets of Barrow-in-Furness, but we didn't seem to make any progress at all. It was almost dusk on November 30th 1930 and the sleet was turning to rain as it drove into our faces. The wind made it feel like buckshot. A small, fat man, Joey Reilly, led us holding the bridle of a little pony pulling a two-wheeled cart. He and the pony were probably as wet and miserable as we were.

On the cart were the worldly possessions of the William Workman family. I remember there were two dolly tubs, stuffed with flock mattresses to keep them dry, a few cardboard boxes of assorted crockery and utensils and some brass bedsteads. That about summed up our worldly goods. Any clothing we possessed we were wearing.

My father walked with one hand on the cart for support, and the other hand holding his walking stick. It was obvious from the way he walked that he was in pain from his false legs, but I think he'd had so much pain he'd learned to live with it. And of course pain-killers were almost unknown in those days – even if they could have been affordable. My elder brother Bill and I trudged along at the back of the cart trying to keep out of the worst of the weather. But this didn't do much good, and we were wet through to the skin and utterly miserable.

We were on our way from Back Harley Street, where we'd lived in a one-up one-down cottage for three months, to our new home in Blake Street, Hindpool. We were going to share a house with a family called Nelson, though how we came to be doing this

I don't know. We were to have the front room downstairs and one bedroom upstairs for the princely sum of two shillings and sixpence a week – paid for by our 'kind' benefactors, the Board of Guardians, or the 'Parish' as they were also known.

Due to the fact that my father was virtually unemployable after the shipyard accident in which he'd lost his legs, he was unable to claim unemployment benefit – such as it was in those 'good old days' – and had to trudge to the Board of Guardians once a week for a voucher worth one pound, plus the two shillings and sixpence in cash for the rent. At that time they operated a system of 'Taskwork', whereby the recipients of this generosity were required to work at the Roose Institution in order to show that they appreciated all that was being done for them . . . but more of that later, I must get back to the story of our welcome in Hindpool, and our first impressions of those people we had come to live amongst.

We finally arrived at the home of Simmy and Sylvia Nelson, who had let part of their house to us. We were ushered into a front room by a girl about a year older than me. My father and both my elder brother and myself were wet through to the skin, hungry and miserable, and at least 'my' teeth were chattering I was so cold and wretched.

Mrs Nelson, our new landlady, took my brother and I under her wing like an old mother hen. I can remember to this day her kindness and solicitude. Within minutes she had all our clothing off and we were wrapped in half blankets, then installed in front of a blazing fire in her room. She disappeared into her kitchen and left us thawing out and wondering where our mother and father were. The next thing I recall was Mrs Nelson reappearing with two tin plates of home made soup for Bill and I. We learned later that it was rabbit stew, and believe me food never tasted so good as it did that day.

People say, "How can you remember incidents like that from so many years ago?" My answer is that apart from our immediate family people were not very benevolent in those days until we came to Hindpool. Simmy Nelson, his wife Sylvia and their two children were, like us, living in the most grinding poverty, and yet what little they had they were willing to share. They were the salt of the earth in their rough-and-ready way, and we were fortunate indeed to share their home. While we were being dried and fed, our father and mother were doing their best to erect beds and make our one bedroom habitable. Jim, our younger brother, meanwhile was being minded by young Sylvia Nelson in the front room, and I'm sure was blissfully unaware of the events going on around him.

Our mother, Maud, and father, William, had meanwhile done all they could to make things as comfortable as possible and had come downstairs. They too were being treated to bowls of the famous 'Nelson Stew' in front of the fire.

We were settling in nicely, and my mother told me later how they had formed an instant rapport with our new hosts, and Simmy, realising instinctively how limited my father was physically, did all he could to make our life a little more bearable. Now, at the end of a long miserable day, we were glad to go to bed and look forward to our stay in Hindpool with a little less foreboding than we'd had all that day.

The following morning my mother took Bill and I to enrol at school; me to the infants and Bill to St James' School. At that time all Hindpool children started their education at Blake Street Infants', and then on to St James' until they left school at fourteen. Another welcome feature at that time in Barrow – I don't know if it was government sponsored, or a local municipal initiative – but we used to start school at 8am in order to have a free breakfast. This was quite a substantial meal of porridge, followed by a different choice each day. In those days, with most people in the same boat, there was no stigma attached to free meals. I think people were more tolerant then, and accepted that the widespread poverty of the early thirties, when there was mass unemployment, was a fact of life and no individual's fault.

So life in Hindpool moved on, and Bill and I made friends at school and gradually came to know most of the 'characters' who lived there.

Grandad Bob had moved with us, but had had to find a lodging, 'bed only', in McClintock Street, the next street to ours, but fortunately the back door to the house he lived in was opposite the back door of ours, so we had him over for most of his meals. At that time he had become very frail, and although we didn't know it of course, he hadn't very long to live.

I thought the world of Grandad Bob. He took me on walks every day after school, and in effect had looked after Bill and me ever since he'd come to live with us in Abbots Mead, because my dad wasn't able to due to his accident.

When I'd first started school aged five, at Cambridge Street Infants' School, it was Grandad Bob who'd taken me in the morning, brought me home for lunch and then collected me when school was over.

Years before, my brother Bill had had an accident when he was about five years old and was unable to walk for almost two years. My mother and he spent a lot of time at the hospital as they made daily visits for dressings etc., so during that time Grandad had been like a father to me. Medical opinion at that time repeatedly begged my mother to agree to amputation, simply because they thought Bill's wounds were incurable. However, my mother steadfastly refused their entreaties so determinedly that one particular doctor asked her why she was so adamant. Her reply was that her husband (our dad) had lost both his legs in an accident in Vickers Armstrong's Shipyard, adding, "And I'll do all in my power to ensure that my son grows up with both legs, and will not have to face the terrible handicap that his dad has had to live with." That particular doctor never asked again, and my mother always said later that this seemed to be a turning point. He renewed his efforts and soon afterwards Bill started to get better.

However, I must get back to those early years in Hindpool. To our young eyes there seemed to be a lot of outstanding 'characters' around, who to us seemed to be larger than life. In retrospect they were probably just men typical of the times they lived in. Those lucky enough to have a job worked long and hard in conditions that wouldn't be tolerated today. I remember men like Pat 'The Wild Man' McLaughlin; the McCready brothers, all local hard men; 'Russian' Bill Clark; Charlie Lindstrom the Swede (an ex-seaman) who we eventually went to live next door to; and 'Little Tommy Wharton' who was quite a useful boxer at local level. Tommy appeared regularly at boxing venues such as the Strand Skating Rink in Barrow, formerly known as the Drill Hall. In those days my father earned an extra shilling or two repairing shoes, and often Tommy would bring his boxing shoes for running repairs (no pun intended). We always knew if he'd won a bout, because he would call and pay my father two shillings and sixpence. On those occasions we always had fish and chips from Whitalls fish & chip shop, so you can imagine we were his most loyal supporters. Sadly, later on in life Tommy went blind, obviously from the punishment he'd taken in the ring.

There were a few more characters, but I'm afraid they don't stand out in my mind as much as those I've mentioned.

At this time, 1931, Mam was pregnant with our sister Sheila, and poor Grandad developed pneumonia. Mam was taken to Roose Infirmary to give birth to Sheila, due to some complication, and Grandad Bob was in the men's ward with the pneumonia from which he died just before Sheila was born – one life ended and another began.

By this time, from what little bit I can remember, added to things said later by other people, relations between my parents and Mr and Mrs Nelson were becoming fraught, although I'm sure there was no acrimony because we remained friendly with them for many years. I think it was just a case of familiarity not exactly breeding contempt, but creating a coolness towards each other through such little chance of privacy.

So Mother decided to look for other accommodation, and eventually found a flat at 303h Duke Street in what were known as 'The Scotch Buildings'. It was occupied at the time by an old lady, Laura Turner, who we came to call Aunt Laura simply from courtesy since she was really no relation at all. She was having great difficulty living on her 'Lloyd George' (state pension), which at that time was a whopping ten shillings a week (fifty pence today). I think she'd been 'wasting' her money on food, and other luxuries like keeping warm etc. Seriously, though, I think she welcomed us more for the company than the extra money. She must have led a lonely life at the top of a block of flats, especially as she had great difficulty climbing the stairs. Sadly, she died twelve months after we moved in. She had no family, and I don't know if anyone attended her funeral or not. What a reflection on society as it was then.

However, before I leave Blake Street behind altogether I'd like to mention a few more of the people who we came to know and like. Next door to us were the Slater family, Ziggy, Nora and two sons Wilf and Charlie. Charlie and I were good friends for many years and went through school together. Wilf, the eldest boy, was killed tragically in the steel works some years later when some molten steel, or slag, was tipped on him.

Ziggy, the father, was a huge man, well over six feet tall. He was an accomplished skater and master of ceremonies at the Strand Rink. He was also the owner of about three whippet dogs, and I think he supplied most of Blake Street with rabbits; a truly welcome source of food at that time.

There was also Mr and Mrs Hubbold, who made and sold home-made sarsaparilla at a penny a bottle, which came with a string round the neck to hold the cork in. Then there were the Fones, the Camerons and the Grahams, all nice people making the best of their lives in very trying circumstances.

I mustn't finish with Blake Street without a word or two about the visits – about once a week – we had from Uncle Alec and Jimmy Connel. Jimmy had a little handcart affair from which he sold ice cream in summer, and paraffin oil etc., in the winter. He, Uncle Alec, and my dad had been friends from schooldays, and when they visited us each week either I or my brother Bill would be sent to Slavins' cake shop with sixpence for as many cakes as possible. I'm afraid we looked for quantity rather than quality and would arrive home with about ten cakes. Jimmy Connel obviously provided the sixpence, and although most of the time life was a struggle I look back on those sort of memories with nostalgic pleasure.

2

Life at 303h Duke Street

I always think of our move to the flat as the start of what I call the
LOCAL NEWS BULLETIN years. My sister Gladys was born in
1933 and so now there were seven of us in a two-roomed flat.
One bedroom for mother and father, and the two girls, and a
curtained recess in the living-room where we lads slept. After our
cramped existence at the Nelson's it seemed palatial. Of course,
it wasn't. My father had great difficulty negotiating the four
flights of stairs, and any services had to be brought up by the
same route. Still, he seemed to cope, although frankly it was
Hobson's choice.

Sometimes when I look back I wonder how my mother kept
her sanity. She was an amazing tower of strength and adaptability,
and over all the trials and tribulations of those harsh days she
retained a sense of humour. And for all the lack of the comforts
which we take for granted today, we were comparatively well fed
and contented due to Mam's initiative and unfailing tolerance.
Years later, an old comrade of mine when describing the ability of
someone he'd known to produce a meal from scant means said:
"She could make a rice pudding out of a dish cloth," and that
about sums up Maud Elsie Workman. The saying could have been
invented for her.

At about this time, approximately 1934, Dad and some like-
minded friends opened the Barrow-in-Furness branch of the
NUWM (National Unemployed Workers' Movement). For some
time he was the secretary, general factotum and treasurer – but,
believe me, there wasn't a lot of 'treasure' about at that time. He

had a few supporters to start off and gradually built up a significant membership which at its peak reached about a hundred. An empty shop was rented in Duke Street, and that became the headquarters for all the important decision making – such as who was to supply the tea, sugar and milk that day – forgive the humour.

For a few short years the NUWM did a lot of good work at local level fighting for what few rights the working class, or rather the 'unworking' class, had at that time. There were meetings on Cavendish Square most Saturday nights – these followed the Salvation Army meetings which always took precedence. Whether these meetings did much good or not is debatable, but at least they raised people's awareness of local issues.

One significant victory achieved by the NUWM resulted in the abolition of the Taskwork, mentioned earlier. Taskwork was a scheme operated not only in Barrow but widely adopted elsewhere. Under this scheme the recipients of an allowance from the Board of Guardians – who at that time in Barrow were situated in a large house in Paradise Street – had to work from nine o'clock to four at the Roose Institute, which was also known as the Workhouse. They were employed in the kitchen gardens or in delivering handcarts of coal from a central supply to various parts of the institution; boiler room, etc. In deference to my father's disability he was given the job of overseer.

In return for this work they were given food vouchers to the value of one pound, which had to be spent in 'their' designated shop. In my father's case, as mentioned earlier, he also received two shillings and sixpence 'cash' to pay his rent. Dad fought hard against the powers that be at that time over the illegality of this scheme, and eventually won a resounding victory in a test case when it 'was' declared illegal.

My father received plaudits from all over the country. I remember one in particular from the Lord Mayor of Hull, which came in the form of a congratulatory telegram, followed by a donation to NUWM funds, which was more than welcome.

Of course, by this time things were afoot in Europe that were to have a profound effect on all our lives. In Italy 'Il Duce' (Benito Mussolini) had ignored world opinion and launched a savage war against Ethiopia. His aim was to create a second

Roman Empire. Adolf Hitler was also flexing his Teutonic muscles in his quest for 'Lebensraum', and to seek revenge for the humiliation of the treaty of Versailles as it was seen in Germany. To German eyes it had been a betrayal, and had to be put right.

Here in Great Britain we had our own home-grown fascists led by Oswald Mosely. Fortunately he only attracted a certain minority, and his provocative marches through London were resisted fiercely by the communist party, who were the only clear voice demonstrating against the evils of fascism. The Government, and certain sections of the aristocracy gave the impression that they were actually in favour of what was going on in Europe. And certainly by their attitude to the two conflicting sides in Spain gave encouragement to Franco and his supporters.

At that time Mosley and his rabble used to publish a newspaper called *Action*. Its distinctive logo was a lightning flash, and one of my jobs (unpaid I might add) was to go to the bookstall kiosk by the Barrow railway station entrance to collect a copy of this scurrilous rag. *Action*, and other newspapers; *Reynolds News*, the *Daily Herald* and the *John Bull Magazine* were always kept on the table in our Duke Street office, and were all regarded as required reading. The membership of the NUWM might have been shabby and ill-fed, but my father saw that they were all well read.

Interestingly, some years later, in the early 1950s, Uncle Alec's wife Aunty Rosie had the tenancy of the kiosk by the station mentioned above, selling tobaccos, sweets etc., and I often saw her there.

At about that time, 1936-37, it was very obvious to intelligent people who didn't bury their heads in the sand, that war was more likely than not. Vickers Armstrong were opening up facilities in the shipyard that had been mothballed for years. As a result, with more jobs about, our little NUWM branch started losing members and soon we had lost our 'raison d'etre'. The end finally came when the Barrow Council built some new public conveniences at Watney, and my father was chosen rather than an able-bodied man to be the attendant. It was the first job he'd had since his accident twenty-five years before.

The imminence of war obviously had a dramatic affect both on our family, and the people we'd lived among for ten eventful

17

years. Before I embark on this part of my memoirs, however, there are one or two interesting and amusing little episodes that are worth recasting, and if I didn't mention them I'd feel I hadn't done justice to the people involved.

During the NUWM years my father had a little coterie of close friends and supporters who as well as being sincere in their beliefs, all helped each other whenever it was necessary. Among them was little Jimmy Creber, a committed socialist who suffered very poor health and had an appalling home life. His mother had died young, and his father was an eccentric tyrant, but like me he tramped miles selling and delivering the *Local News Bulletin* which my father produced on an old Roneo duplicator. This bulletin was simply what its name said, a 'local news source', and as such at that time it was very popular. My father pulled no punches and exposed quite a few shady deals concerning contracts and local councillors. Little Jimmy, despite his health and home problems, did quite a lot of the leg-work, verifying etc., that Dad wasn't capable of.

Then there was Jimmy Weir, a huge man but a very kindly person, and also extremely loyal. He had a quaint, old fashioned manner of speaking and always addressed my mother as 'Mistress' Workman. He made a point of going around second-hand shops, and if he spotted anything that my mother could alter or adapt, shirts or trousers etc, that could be cut to fit one of us, he'd bring it to her. I'm afraid that at the time we certainly didn't appreciate her efforts at all. Our unspoken dread was that Mr Weir would pass on his *own* cast-offs, particularly because he was given to wearing an old pair of jodhpurs that he'd bought cheap somewhere. Fortunately it never came to that.

Another old character who helped with *Bulletin* chores was a chap named Alec. I've forgotten his surname, but he claimed to have been in the army with Bombardier Billy Wells, and to have acted as his trainer and coach. He seemed genuine enough, and all his stories seemed to match up. Bombardier Billy Wells, of course, had been a British heavyweight boxing champion from 1911 to 1919, and it was he who, after his boxing days were over, was eventually hired by J. Arthur Rank to strike the huge gong at the start of the Rank Studio films.

All these people were part of our lives during the thirties, and I can only say that they made life at least more colourful in their various ways.

I think, looking back, that our household must have been unique in the fact that conversation revolved around such international political and revolutionary people as 'Bela Kun', 'Rosa Luxembourg', 'Appassionaria', 'Maurice Thorez', and others, who in their own particular fashion had all attempted, sometimes futilely, to alter and make things better for their fellow men.

For those unfamiliar with these names from those troubled inter-war years here is a brief clarification:

(1) **BELA KUN** was the leader of the Hungarian Socialist Party, and fought valiantly to break the stranglehold of a reactionary clique that ruled Hungary in the aftermath of the First World War. However, his efforts were in vain. It must be remembered that at this period in time all the old certainties that had obtained prior to 1914 had been swept away. All over Europe there seemed to be a growing dawning of intelligence that life could be better than it had been, and Bela Kun was in the forefront of that struggle, vainly of course.

(2) **ROSA LUXEMBOURG** was a dedicated communist, who was also prominent in the fight to create a better life for ordinary people. It too was doomed to fail, the forces of 'reaction' are very strong.

(3) **APPASSIONARIA** was a power in the Republican Movement in Spain. Her exploits were as legendary as her name was, and she lived to see her arch-enemy Franco die and his hated Falangists treated with the disdain they deserved.

(4) **MAURICE THOREZ** was at that time a fervent socialist who went on to become leader of the French Communist Party.

Of course some of these people were probably misguided in certain respects, but were at least sincere in their beliefs, and possessed an unwavering belief in the justice of their actions.

When I look back to those days in the early thirties I feel privileged to have grown up among people who believed passionately that if socialism in its true application was not the answer to poverty and wasted lives, then there is no answer at all.

Whatever else our childhood did it left me personally with an abiding abhorrence of those who manipulate positions of power and influence for their own benefit, whilst purporting to have their constituents' interests at heart.

And now finally the last, but certainly not the least, of the people who have a special place in my memory, is our Aunty Bessie. She was my father's sister, and due to her mother having died young, poor Aunty Bessie was sent to relatives in Scotland to be brought up. I don't know the circumstances of her childhood, but I should imagine they were far better than if she'd stayed in Barrow. However, grow up she did and eventually married Uncle Jack. They settled in Bradford, and had four children. To me they seemed to be quite comfortably off, and I had two unforgettable holidays with them. The first time I stayed for a week, and the second almost three weeks. I've never known the reason that 'I' was chosen to go and not any of my brothers or sisters, but at the time that was the last of my worries.

During my stays my aunt and uncle were kindness and solicitude personified, and I always thought a great deal of them. My cousins, however, who were all older than I was, gave me the impression that they had their own lives to live. Consequently I was left to my own devices most of the time. Luckily I was always quite content in my own company, and I enjoyed myself immensely roaming around Bradford, hopping on and off their superb tramway system.

During the thirties Aunty Bessie came through to Barrow quite often, and always brought a welcome supply of food, etc. We looked forward to her visits and I think to us lads she was a cross between Lady Bountiful and Mother Theresa. She thought a great deal of my mother and always brought her a little personal treat on her visits. She was a lovely person.

3

Time to Earn a Living

By this time, about 1937, I started work as a milkboy delivering for the Co-operative Society. My wage was a princely 7/6d per week with a deduction of 5d for an insurance stamp. In today's money this is approximately 37½p. Still, it was a welcome addition to household finances. To show it in its true perspective, at that time a hundredweight of best coal was 1/6d, and twenty Players Cigarettes 11½d, so really it was all quite relative.

My older brother, Bill, had been working at the local candle works, and I found out later that his working conditions were pretty primitive. He also earned about eight shillings a week. But being ever inventive, he'd smuggle what were known as mis-shapes out of the factory, and although there was only the one gas mantle in our flat, due to Bill's initiative we were lit up like an operating theatre.

Jim, my younger brother, was still at school and the lasses, Sheila and Gladys, were growing up nicely, little realising that in three short years we'd all be scattered to different places.

I think, looking back on that particular time, we seemed to be better off and certainly more content than we had been as a family for a long time. Dad was working, Bill and I were bringing home a few shillings, and I don't think Mam had that same sense of desperation she'd had for years to provide meals and all the necessities for a large family.

At that time a rather good repertory company was in residence at His Majesty's Theatre in Barrow. They were very popular and my mother and I went every Friday night until they had exhausted their repertoire. *Charlie's Aunt* and *Night Must Fall* by Emlyn Williams were her favourites, but she enjoyed all their other offerings as well. She looked forward to those evenings out. Two seats cost a shilling, plus another sixpence for sweets, and we'd had a decent, entertaining experience.

The leading light of the 'Terence Byron Repertory Company' was an actor called Richard Thompson, who was unfortunately killed in the RAF during the war. A sad loss. My mother ranked him alongside Olivier.

So taking things all round we seemed to be getting over the worst of the previous lean years. One example on my second Christmas as a milk boy with the Co-op – most Barrovians pronounced it as 'Cope' – was the amount of tips I received as Christmas boxes, I had well over four pounds in coppers and sixpences, etc., so I must have been more popular than I'd imagined. Either that or the customers felt sorry for me.

At any rate we had the best Christmas we'd ever had, though alas it was also the last. By the following Christmas, Bill would be in the army, having gone off to Kendal recruiting office and volunteered. How he'd passed the medical remains a mystery to this day, because he was seventy-five per cent blind in his left eye. However, he was accepted and served the war years in the Grenadier Guards.

By this time I'd teamed up with a pal and we presented ourselves at what was known as the Labour Market at Barrow's Ramsden Dock. More and more ships were arriving at Barrow due, of course, to the imminence of war. Mostly they had cargoes of pit props for the coal mines, or pulp wood for Barrow's paper mill, and iron ore and scrap metal for the steel and iron works.

The hiring foreman, dubious at first over our ages, eventually, because of a shortage of older labour, gave us a chance and I think he was pleasantly surprised. What we lacked in years we made up for in enthusiasm and we were quick learners. The added incentive from my point of view was seeing the ships and lifestyle of the crews. I knew instinctively from then on, that at the first opportunity I had I was going to be a merchant seaman. I'd always longed to see what was on the other side of the hill, and at sixteen this looked like my chance.

However, I'd like to go back and recall a few other people who had a profound effect on our early lives, and who I seem to have overlooked.

Before our move from Back Hartington Street to Hindpool in 1930 (where I began this story), we'd lived for about seven years in another part of Barrow called Abbotsmead. While we were there my mother did odd jobs for a Mrs Dixon who had a little sweet shop in Friars Lane – a little cleaning and, on occasion, minding the shop. They became firm friends, and although Jessie, as she was called, had a rather annoying habit of presenting herself as superior to the rest of the people, she also had a heart of gold, and she and my mother, who could accept her hauteur and ignore it, remained friends for life.

Jessie Dixon had two lovely daughters, Dorothy the elder and Marjory the younger, both of whom died from pneumonia within a week of each other in the harsh winter of 1941. What a loss. The poor woman was absolutely distraught, and without my mother's kindly ministrations she herself would probably have died. In actual fact she outlived my mother.

My father, however, never actually cared for Mrs Dixon regardless of her kindness. You see, she used lipstick, and in 1930's Barrow that was the height of decadence. How times change.

Another person I remember vividly was the conservative councillor: Mrs Edie Ann Ward. Her husband had a plumbing business in Dalton Road, T.Ward & Sons – I think it still exists. How strange that the contracts for council work would nearly always go to him . . ? I would *never* suggest that it was because his wife was an influence. I merely comment on the coincidence.

Councillor Ward's political opinions were slightly to the right of 'Vlad the Impaler', and I think if she'd had her own way she would have had an annual cull of all those members of society who'd reached the end of their usefulness. Obviously she was a target for the *Local News Bulletin*, and my father lampooned her mercilessly. He nicknamed her 'Nausea Bagwash', and she in turn reviled him at every opportunity. But, and this is the reason I mention her at all, she'd known my mother since Mam was a girl in 'service', as it was known. In those days working girls lived in the big houses enduring long hours of drudgery for a pittance of a wage plus their food and lodgings. And before Mam married Dad she'd done a stint for Mrs Ward, who'd been impressed by her hard work and reliability. Apparently she'd told Mam that if she was ever in any difficulties over the coming years she was to let her know immediately. On more than one occasion I was sent to the posh house in Prospect Road, where she lived, with a sealed note. And although I never knew at the time that it was a request for financial assistance, never once did she make me feel small. And invariably I left with pockets full of fruit, etc., and something in an envelope for Mam. What a paradox some people are. They apparently call this 'noblesse oblige', and Mrs Ward had it in abundance.

There are others who I remember fondly, and others who I prefer to forget, so I'll get on with the rest of my story from where the war was approaching, became a reality, and how we played our part in the downfall of 'Adolf Schickelgruber' by opening up the 'Workman Offensive'. Somehow I don't think that at the time it gave 'Adolf' any sleepless nights, or altered the course of the war by one iota. Still, we tried.

Bill, my older brother, was the first to go, and on the day he left for Wellington Barracks in London I remember that my mother was inconsolable. I think she thought that after all her valiant efforts to ensure he reached manhood and despite all his many setbacks, here he was going to be shot by some nameless Jerry, whose own mother probably thought on the same lines.

Dad was more practical. He knew it was inevitable that we'd all either volunteer or be conscripted into one or other of the services, and told me to at least try to choose the one I wanted to be in. As I've said earlier, this presented no problems for me, as I knew that I was going into the Merchant Marine as it was then known. I think it was later altered to the Merchant Navy so as to give the powers that be some semblance of authority over what was, after all, a civilian service. Early on in the war there were to be attempts to force us to sign articles and wear a uniform, but these failed. I think that one of the factors which eventually caused the volte-face was the horrendous loss of life and shipping that the first two years of the war brought. One in five of all merchant seamen lost their lives in the course of the war, and millions of tons of badly needed shipping were sunk. When I look back I always think of the words of the German song that said:

'No Roses Bloom On A Sailor's Tomb,
And No Lilies Wave on An Ocean Grave.'

4

The Call of the Sea

Still, I'm getting ahead of myself . . . At this time, August 1939, I was only a worker at Ramsden Docks.

My dad was prescient as usual. He'd always said that when this war came, it was as inevitable as night following day that it would mean as much to innocent civilians in their homes as it would to the fighting men. I think he'd taken the bombing of Guernica during the Spanish Civil War as a portent of what was to come. Once again he was proved right. The bombing of civilians by 'both' protagonists was in my opinion both unnecessary and, as events have shown since, futile. All it ever achieved on both sides was to stiffen the victim's resolve, and it didn't shorten the war by one day. It simply inflicted death, pain and destruction on a scale never experienced before by innocent people who did not deserve it.

By this time all the local lads of twenty were being called up, and by one test or another were being sent off to join one of the services. Many of them, and I suspect 'more' than not, were to be square pegs in round holes. Sadly, many of them would never see Hindpool again, while some were to return wounded or blind, and most of the rest would have experiences that would remain with them for the rest of their lives.

At this time, just prior to the outbreak of war, my so-called 'casual' job at Ramsden Dock, had become virtually full-time employment. It paid well, giving me more money than I'd ever had. I was sixteen years old, and there I was being paid the same twelve shillings and sixpence as everyone else for a nine-hour

b

day. In today's decimal money it was approximately sixty-five pence, but to me then it was a veritable fortune. Sadly I think it went to my head.

Then came the day that Chamberlain came on the radio and made the shock announcement that we were at war with Germany.

When I look back I can't remember having any sense of foreboding, and once the initial excitement had worn off, things seemed to carry on as usual. Of course, there was the blackout, and the inevitable shortages in the shops, but I think on the whole that people were lulled into a false feeling of, 'It'll all be over soon. Our lads would give Jerry a bloody good hiding and that would be that.' How wrong we all were.

My mother was dreading the very thought of war, she'd been a young woman during the first blood-bath in 1914–18 and saw the cream of the nation's youth cut down in their prime. Now she had three sons of her own who would all be of an age to get involved. Another tragic consequence was the thought of her two little girls having to be evacuated to what were thought of as places of safety in the country.

It wasn't until years later that I realised what a hammer-blow it must have been to her. Her entire family scattered miles from home, and her youngest, Sheila and Gladys, being sent off to live with people who were not only strangers, but in the event not very kind either. The billeting of these unlucky kids was in fact forced on these 'foster parents', and some of them made little attempt to welcome, reassure or comfort them. Some were very considerate, of course, but I'm afraid many were not. Added to this was the fact that these 'places of safety' were of necessity in the most isolated and inaccessible areas, and no help was given to mothers who wanted to visit their children.

However, back now to my attempts to become a sailor, and my introduction to a certain Pieder Manjon Pedreaux, a Norwegian master mariner and captain of the SS *Fidelio*.

In November 1939 a gang of us, about ten in all, were sent to unload a ship in what was called the Anchor-line Basin at Ramsden Docks. The SS *Fidelio* was a typical four-thousand ton tramp steamer. She'd arrived the day before with a cargo of pit props from Finland for the coal mines of Lancashire and Cumberland, and was apparently lucky to have avoided hostile

26

Jerry attacks all the way. When her holds were opened it was realised that there weren't cranes strong enough at her present berth to discharge her cargo, so the powers that be decided to take the ship back into Ramsden Dock proper, where there were better facilities. The trouble was that there was now no deck crew left on board to handle the mooring ropes etc for this move, as they'd all been granted leave on arrival in Barrow. Only the captain, the chief officer and the second officer remained, therefore moving the ship was going to be a problem.

While the matter was being discussed two small tugs arrived to tow the *Fidelio* to her new berth in Ramsden Dock. To save time and money a decision had to be made, and the charge-hand of our dock worker's squad asked the mate, or Chief Officer as he was officially known, if we could help by taking the place of the deck crew. The second mate then went into a huddle with the first mate and the captain, and they agreed. The first mate would take five of us forward to handle the bow moorings and the tug rope, while the others with the second mate would look after the stern moorings, etc.

Both officers had a fair command of English, and with their clear, lucid orders the whole operation went off smoothly. About forty minutes later we were tied up in the new berth ready to start unloading the cargo. During all this I'd had the strangest feeling of what I can only describe as 'exhilaration'. For the first time in my life I'd been afloat on a moving vessel, and even though it was only from one dock to another, I'd enjoyed the experience immensely.

The following day we returned to unload her cargo and after about eight days the ship was empty, and except for taking on supplies of coal for her stoke holds, food, etc, she was ready for sea again. She'd had only a short respite, and was now effectively part of the allied war effort; her link with Norway severed for a while.

Her sailing day was set, and her crew started to return one by one. However, forty-eight hours before she was due to leave three of the crew were still missing, and there seemed to be no Norwegian replacements in Great Britain.

This was the chance I think I'd been waiting for, although at the time I didn't believe it would work. In our squad there was an Irish lad whose family had moved to Barrow some years before, and who, like me, was keen to become a sailor. I think we decided that fortune favoured the brave – or fools rush in where wise men fear to go. However, we approached the second mate whose English was quite good, and told him that if possible we were both very eager to go to sea. And though we had no credentials of any sort we were quick learners, and were ready to sign on with a minimum of fuss now that they were short handed.

I think his initial reaction was one of astonishment, but at least he didn't dismiss us both out of hand. After letting what I'd said sink in, he indicated that we were to follow him up to the bridge deck and the captain's quarters. This, as I've said earlier, was where I met Captain Pieder Manjon Pedreaux, of the Norwegian Merchant Marine.

The second mate knocked at the door just behind the bridge and went in leaving us outside. What went on in there I don't know, but after about ten minutes the door opened and we were shown into what was a sort of sitting-room. The captain was seated at a desk writing something in a ledger, and after what seemed an age, but was probably only minutes, he looked up and stared at us both as if he could see through us. I think at the time I realised he was one of that breed of men who are born to be in command. We certainly thought that this man would stand no nonsense and we didn't intend to upset him.

Finally he spoke, first to me and then to Pat, my pal. He said that the second mate had been impressed by the way we had helped to move the ship from one berth to another. He also said that the missing crewmen would not be returning, as they'd already joined another ship.

He then spoke to the second mate in Norwegian and we were shepherded out of the captain's quarters and told to go back to our offloading job; we would be given the captain's decision the following day.

The next day we were there at 8am, all agog for the captain's verdict. We were not disappointed. The second mate was waiting for us at the top of the gangway with instructions. We were to go to the office of O.M. Huartsons in Hindpool Road, who were the ship's official representatives and also consul for Norway. Here we were to be officially signed on as members of the crew of the SS *Fidelio*.

It was quite a short affair, and at 11.30am on the 12th

November 1939 I had left civilian life behind, and to all intents and purposes I was now a merchant seaman.

Captain Pedreaux then made us sign a document, after which we were told to present ourselves at Tooner & Denisons Outfitters in Ramsden Dock Road where a line of credit had been opened up for the Irish boy and myself. We were to equip ourselves with what are now known as jeans, but were then called dungarees, plus thick sweaters, thick long-johns underwear, socks, a pair of wellington boots, and a full-length oilskin coat.

The manager of the shop asked me my name, and when I told him he said he knew my mother very well as a customer, and asked to be remembered to her. At the time I didn't know that I wouldn't be able to pass on this message until almost two years into the future.

Our bill for all the gear was just over five pounds each. Apparently the ship's agents would foot this, and then of course it would be stopped off our wages at the end of the voyage.

We then proceeded to join the ship, and to be shown our cabins and meet our new shipmates. By this time it was almost four o'clock in the afternoon, and we were to sail on the tide at ten o'clock that evening.

5

Down to the Sea in Ships

When I look back on that first day, I think I believed I was going to wake up at any moment and find it was all a dream. I was soon to wake up to reality. Pat and I were given half an hour to settle in with our belongings, then the second mate, who also acted as the bosun in charge of the deck crew, assigned two of the Norwegian lads to take us on deck and show us the rudiments of battening down the hatches and getting the ship ready for sea. Everything, we found, had to be stowed away or lashed down with ropes so that in the event of bad weather all was secure.

I was very fortunate in that the able seaman who was put in charge of me spoke faultless English. I was already beginning to understand that all the rubbish I'd been told about the British superiority over 'Johnny foreigner' was just that, rubbish! Here was a Norwegian seaman of only twenty years of age and yet he was able to speak English as well as I could.

His name was Kaare (pronounced Cora) Gunderson, and as time went on his assistance was invaluable. He taught me to handle ropes and mooring wires, to splice, and tie all the various knots so essential to a deckhand's life at sea. I think that with his help I gradually became an efficient seaman – self-praise indeed.

Our sailing time approached and shortly before ten the pilot came aboard to guide us down the channel to the open sea. His arrival was followed by the two tugs again. We passed tow wires to the tugs and let go our shore moorings. My career as a sailor had now really begun.

After being manoeuvred out of the docks the tugs were

released, and under the guidance of the pilot we started off down the Walney Channel. We sailed past Roa Island, and then shortly afterwards the pilot shook hands with the captain and boarded the pilot cutter wishing us all 'Bon Voyage'. At last we were on our own. I think I had crossed my rubicon, and was now a seaman; albeit a very young and inexperienced one. Of course, only time could alter that.

Our first destination was Ardrossan in Scotland, where we would load coal for our bunkers; the SS *Fidelio*'s engines were coal fired and she needed some hundreds of tons to cross the Atlantic and, of course, bring her back again. Bunkering was a dirty, messy business as the coal dust penetrated everywhere, and after it was completed it took hours with hose pipes to clean the ship up.

By this time I was feeling very tired, mainly through lack of sleep due to our accommodation being in the stern of the vessel where the vibration of the 'screw' (propeller) had even my 'teeth' chattering. Fortunately, up to now the weather had been comparatively mild, and apart from a slight queasiness I hadn't been seasick.

It was now a week since we'd left Barrow, and slowly but surely we were settling into some sort of routine. We were due to sail from Ardrossan to Gourock at the mouth of the Clyde to join a convoy at seven o'clock that evening.

At about six o'clock the chief officer came to my cabin and told me to report at once to the captain's cabin. I was frightened out of my wits. I thought 'what the hell have I done to be summoned like this?' I could see all my efforts turning out to be in vain.

When I presented myself to the bridge, the captain was with a rather large Scottish police sergeant, and to me they both looked rather grim. It appeared that my poor mother, so upset at my virtually running away to sea, had tried to have me declared under age and returned home. To my relief the police sergeant asked me if I was quite content to remain on board, and when I assured him I was, that was that. I think the captain was as relieved as I was, he wanted no more disruption with his crew. What my mother thought about the result I can only guess, but of course she came to terms with it eventually.

At seven o'clock on a cold November evening we sailed from

Ardrossan to the convoy marshalling anchorage known as, 'The Tail of The Bank', at the mouth of the Clyde, and arrived still in darkness the following morning.

When daylight came it seemed a miracle to me how Captain Pedreaux had manoeuvred the ship in a strict blackout to his appointed anchorage without a mishap of any kind. As I've said before, he truly was a Master Mariner.

We had put an accommodation ladder over the side, and later on that day a naval tender came alongside and two officers were closeted with the captain and chief officer for about an hour. As was rightly assumed by all, they had come to give us our orders. Of course rumours were ten a penny, and all the older crew members knew *exactly* where we were bound for. We found out later that they were all wrong. Even the captain hadn't been told, he'd simply been given sealed orders that were not to be opened until we were at sea in convoy.

The rest of that day was a whirl of activity. A small coaster came alongside and we took on supplies of food, etc, and were kept busy carrying it all to the storerooms. By the amount we brought aboard I thought we must be going away for about seven years. The coaster was followed by a water tanker which passed hoses aboard to top up our fresh water supply. At long last we were ready for sea, and it was only a matter of waiting for orders.

Among the items the supply ship had brought were about ten five-gallon drums of battleship grey paint, and from daylight to dusk we painted everything above decks dark grey. I was gradually learning that being a sailor entailed more than Errol Flynn had led me to believe. I'd been under the impression it would be all singing sea shanties to an old melodeon and muttering, "Ah . . ! Jim lad," with one eye closed. I couldn't have been more wrong

By this time the anchorage had filled up with ships of all descriptions, and there seemed to be an air of expectancy about. The same naval vessel that had brought our previous orders came alongside again, but this time only delivered a leather briefcase. Whatever it contained must have been instructions on how to join the convoy.

The engine-room had been on stand-by for days and it didn't take the engineers and stokers long to get ready for a voyage. Our anchor was raised and our bow headed out to sea, we were to join our convoy.

The convoy system, we learned, was an attempt to minimise losses of ships vulnerable to U-boat attack, particularly old tramp steamers like ours with a top speed of about ten knots an hour – much less when the weather was bad. About forty or more ships would form up in lanes, usually about four, with each ship following the one in front. They would then zig-zag across the Atlantic in a way that almost doubled the length of the journey. On the outside of the convoy destroyers and other naval ships would patrol up and down, theoretically to protect the merchant ships. These destroyers, corvettes, etc., did an amazingly heroic job, sometimes in truly appalling conditions, but sadly not always successfully; the odds were too much against them.

The losses of ships and men of the merchant navy in those first years of the war were beyond belief. They were nothing more than sitting ducks, and the enthusiasm of the submarine captains to send their fellow sailors to a watery grave was, in my opinion, appalling. I personally think that submarine warfare, by whoever wages it, is an obscenity and should be banned as is poison-gas.

At least a surface enemy is visible, prone to counter attack and doesn't skulk hundreds of feet beneath the sea to launch a sneak attack on an unsuspecting foe. It is a sneaky, underhand method of warfare. Of course, the U-boat skippers and crew were fêted as heroes when they returned to Germany, as were our own submariners. I hope they all had nightmares as they contemplated the results of their handiwork . . . I myself was later to suffer as a result of this type of activity, and it's a ghastly experience when your world sinks beneath you.

After our departure from Glasgow we set off out into the Atlantic, and as we did so I learned that in the wheel-house of every ship in the convoy there was a clock with adjustable brass pointers. These were set at different points on the clock face according to a prearranged timetable. Naturally the clock on every ship was synchronised and as the minute hand touched one of these pointers there would be a pronounced buzz, and the officer on watch would dictate a new course to the man at the wheel. Then 'as one ship' the whole convoy would turn either to port or starboard. In theory this was to baffle the unseen U-boats in the wolf pack, making it difficult for them to work out the correct direction to fire their torpedoes. All of these precautions must have done *some* good, because experience was to prove that without the convoy system the losses of men and ships would undoubtedly have been colossal.

Slowly but surely we zig-zagged our way across the Atlantic to Halifax, Nova Scotia, Canada, which due to its geographical position and natural advantages had become the convoy base for arrivals from, and departures to, the United Kingdom.

We dropped anchor in the harbour to await further orders, and the captain, realising how weary we all were after such a hazardous voyage, detailed two men to keep watch on the bridge then sent the rest of the crew below to get a well earned rest while the ship lay at anchor waiting.

The following morning I was up early as I still had all my chores to do, and while I was cleaning the windows on the bridge and sweeping up in general, a motor launch drew alongside and a Canadian official came aboard. He was shown to the captain's quarters, and after about an hour the captain, chief officer and chief engineer, all resplendent in their best uniforms, left the ship in the launch, heading for the quayside.

They were ashore about seven to eight hours and when they returned all seemed to be quite merry. Of course, being a ship rumour was rife, as usual. However, all was made clear when we were told that we were all to be allowed ashore the next day for about eight hours.

6

Ashore in the 'New World'

The launch turned up at about ten o'clock the next morning and away we went. We'd been allowed to draw five Canadian dollars each, which at that time was worth about one pound, ten shillings. My Irish mate Kaare Gunderson and I decided we would stick together, and with the help of Kaare's experience we knew we'd have a great day.

And so I set foot ashore in my first foreign country – even though everyone in it spoke English. Our first visit was to a 'drugstore', to sample the delights of their ice cream parlours. I don't remember what it was we ordered, but if I'd have ordered it in England it would have cost a fortune, all I remember is that it was marvellous. And what was even better, when the owner of the drugstore found out we were from the convoy in the harbour he wished us well and refused all payment.

All in all we had a wonderful day ashore, one I remember especially for the kindness of the Canadians we met. When we eventually returned to the ship with our bags of souvenirs for home, we had about ten cents left between us, but were over the moon with our day out.

The following day we received instructions to sail to Sidney, Cape Breton, which was 200 miles to the north in order to replenish our coal stocks – obviously depleted by the tortuous voyage from the UK. So we left Halifax in our wake, next stop Sidney, and then to who knows where?

On arrival in Sidney, Cape Breton we were piloted straight to the coal loading berth, where the whole dirty business of bunkering began again. As usual the dust got everywhere, making life just about as unpleasant as it gets. But, as Al Jolson used to say, 'You ain't heard nothin' yet', because when our next orders came we learned that we'd been detailed to make two trips to Montreal, ferrying, of all things, coal . . ! Obviously we wouldn't be crossing the Atlantic again for some time. It seemed that this job was necessary because ships loading and unloading in Montreal were having to divert to Sidney to refuel, so it was our job to build up a stockpile in Montreal to save them all these diversionary trips.

This coal shuttling actually went on for about seven weeks during which we never seemed to be clean. When it finally came to an end the relief all round was tremendous, not least because by this time the Canadian winter was setting in, and each trip was becoming worse than the last. I think our captain was particularly anxious to get away before the snows came.

Our next sailing orders were to St John, New Brunswick, where we would load a cargo of timber for the UK. At last we would be homeward bound, and I must confess that now the initial euphoria had worn off, I was beginning to be homesick myself. I felt sorry for the rest of the crew who had left Norway at the outbreak of war. They wouldn't see their homeland and loved ones for many years. Some, sadly, would never return.

As I remember it took almost two weeks to load our cargo of timber in New Brunswick. All the holds were full and we also had a deck cargo of other kinds of timber. At last we were ready for sea, and we now had to return to Halifax to join our east bound convoy for home and another perilous crossing of the Atlantic.

Before I go on to the actual trip, where we lost a third of the convoy to a wolf pack of U-boats, I'd like to say a little about my shipmates who, as would be expected, made a lasting impression on me. The Irish lad who'd joined with me in Barrow had turned out to be not a very nice chap at all. While *I* made every effort to get on with most of the crew, Pat seemed to go out of his way to antagonise them. He'd scoff at their attempts to speak broken English, and call them turnip heads etc. He had such a truculent attitude that I'm afraid he took quite a few back-handers for his insolence, and if it hadn't been for myself he wouldn't have had a friend on board the ship.

Amongst the crew, who were mostly Norwegian of course,

were two Swedes and a Hungarian of about forty-five who'd married a Norwegian girl and settled in Oslo, the capital of Norway. He was one of the most interesting people I've met before or since. He seemed to be fluent in any language he happened to come across. His English was faultless, and he talked quite well in all the Scandinavian tongues. During our time in Canada he talked to French Canadians at ease. He'd spent time in most European cities over the last twenty years, and would describe experiences that held us all spellbound. Apart from all else he was a master story teller. Years later I heard that he'd survived the war and returned safely to Oslo.

The rest of the crew were quite ordinary, competent sailors and engineers who didn't stand out in any way, except that for the most part they were helpful and kindly disposed. The one 'far from ordinary' exception I must give mention to was the captain. He was only about five foot six inches tall, but about the same in width. He was around sixty years old, grizzled in appearance and the image of the old film star Edward G. Robinson. I think it would have been a foolish man who crossed him in his younger days. He told me on bridge watch one night that his father had been master of an old windjammer in the days of sail, and that he himself had started his sea-going career in 1890 when he was about ten years old, and had sailed all through the First World War without a mishap. I fervently hoped that his luck would continue for the rest of *this* war.

All through the long voyage home, no matter what watch was on, I never saw him leave the bridge, I think he must have slept standing up. During the worst of the U-boat attacks he showed no emotion, and I'm sure his outward appearance of calm gave all of us confidence.

I admired him very much, though I'm afraid he was one of a dying breed. The command of the 'Old *Fidelio*' seemed to be his life, although I knew he had a family back home in Norway and supposed that when his ship was safely in port he would return to being a more relaxed individual.

We left Halifax on the 11th of April 1940, and immediately ran into thick fog, which was frightening as we could show no lights because of blackout restrictions. I remembered that it was my older brother Bill's birthday, and wondered where he was at that stage of the war. I hoped he wasn't as cold and miserable as I was at that moment.

Each ship in the convoy lane had to tow a fog buoy. This was a device that threw up a spume of water as it was towed through the sea, so that the lookouts on the bow of the following ship could see it and make sure they didn't creep up on the ship in front and collide. This lookout duty was a lousy job, you were wet through to the skin and after two hours peering into the thick fog to keep an eye on the buoy in front, the eyes felt as though they were full of sand.

Eventually the leading ship of the convoy decided to turn south to escape the fog and as the day wore on we came out of it – what a relief that was. Now, apart from zig-zagging like mad, there was only three-thousand miles of ocean and a few U-boats between us and home.

By the third or fourth of May we were somewhere off the north of Ireland. It was blowing a living gale with blinding sleet; winter giving us a reminder of what it was still capable of.

The voyage from Halifax, Nova Scotia, in Canada had been a nightmare. We'd lost eleven ships from a convoy of thirty-eight. It didn't seem to matter what course we took, and we were changing course as many as ten times an hour, the U-boats stuck to us like limpets. Somewhere between Greenland and Iceland seemed to be the worst.

I say we 'lost' eleven ships, but of course that wasn't how it was; they'd been savagely destroyed by an invisible, cowardly enemy, who'd sent decent seafaring men and boys to the bottom of the Atlantic. And these monsters were called heroes back in Germany. I don't for one second deny the fact that these men were brave, they must have been to endure the conditions of life aboard a submarine, I just think their bravery was misplaced. They say that all's fair in love and war, but to me and my old shipmates this was butchery on a barbarous scale.

At 4am, on what turned out to be that fateful morning, the 12am to 4am watch was changing over with the new 4am to 8am watch who were coming on duty to take over lookout duties. I was fast asleep in my bunk as my watch didn't start until 8am – having finished my previous watch at midnight and broken all records to get to bed, all I'd taken off were my rubber boots and my heavy watch coat. I think I was asleep by 12.15am.

At approximately 4.15am the stern of the ship, where our

cabins were, suddenly seemed to lift about ten feet in the air and then sink down again. Next there came a series of loud bangs followed by a long, protracted metallic scraping noise.

All those who were in their bunks were bounced around like dice in a cup. And as soon as we'd gathered our scattered wits together, we grabbed what clothing we could, plus a life jacket, and scrambled up on deck as fast as possible.

Apart from the wind and rain there was an eerie silence in the ship. The engines had stopped and we seemed to be listing heavily to starboard (the right-hand side). Our deck cargo of timber had slipped, causing the ship to heel right over. I think at that moment every one of us feared the worst. Would we have to abandon ship? I believe now that if we'd had to take to the boats in that weather there would have been a lot of casualties.

Quickly we began to realise the predicament we were in. With every roll of the ship the deck cargo seemed to groan louder; the binding chains were all that was holding it together, and in the pitch darkness we could only surmise how bad things were. We dare not show a light although the convoy was miles away by now. Prior to the deck cargo slipping there'd been a temporary gangway from the stern of the ship to the midships area, but now with the slipped deck cargo we on the stern were isolated, and until daylight nothing could be done about it.

Between the gusts of wind the chief officer shouted across to us through a megaphone from the top of the bridge deck. At the time I couldn't understand what he said as he shouted in Norwegian. Translated later, I learned he was explaining that whatever had caused our catastrophe had damaged the propeller and rudder, and consequently we were drifting helplessly. The most fortunate factor at that minute was that the wind wasn't blowing us towards the nearby coast. So if we were lucky enough to stay afloat, when daylight came someone would come out to our assistance. Until then all we could do was hope.

There were fourteen of us on the stern of the ship; everyone else was amidships or in the engine-room. One of the Norwegian seaman with us was a huge chap about thirty-five called Nils. He was a decent, sensible man who took charge, thankfully, and made everyone take shelter down below. He had two theories as to what had happened, but of course they were only theories. His first was that a torpedo had struck us a glancing blow, and, luckily

39

for us, had only exploded afterwards. His second was that we had crashed across a submerged U-boat, and the scraping noises were the conning tower under our rudder and propeller. If that were true, it came to me later, we'd probably be the only old tramp steamer to sink a U-boat without firing a shot. At the time, though, we were all scared to death. I know I was, and simply longing for daylight and some form of rescue.

At long last dawn came, and thankfully the wind and rain seemed to go with the night. The gangway across the top of the deck cargo of timber had miraculously survived, although to me it looked very shaky. Nils, our unspoken leader, then asked me – being the smallest and, he assumed, the most agile – to cross this gangway to the middle section of the ship. I think the reason I agreed was vanity, certainly not bravery. I couldn't let the rest know that I was dreading it, so I meekly said yes to hide my fear. He gave me the end of a light rope which they would use to drag a stronger rope across, to give the rest of them a sort of life-line from stern to amidships. Off I went, and almost before I knew it I'd reached the other side to be grabbed by the second mate and pulled to the relative safety of the lower bridge. They soon set up the heavy life-line and within minutes everyone was across and making for the galley and a warm drink.

Shortly afterwards a naval ship (a frigate I think) hove into view. It appeared we'd been missed, and the convoy commodore (leader) feared the worst and had sent the frigate to look for survivors. When he learned of our inability to steer, he weighed up the situation and went off somewhere to get assistance.

This came in the shape of a large trawler/converted-mine-sweeper, which took a wire tow rope from us and set off to the south. It was great to be on the move again, even though it wasn't under our own steam.

It must have been about ten hours later that we were towed into what turned out to be Lough Foyle in Northern Ireland. We then let go our tow line, and dropped anchor almost a mile from Moville in the Irish Free State, as it was then known. It was strange to see all the lights fully lit on the one side of the Lough, and on the other a full blackout – one of the paradoxes of war, but of course the Free State remained neutral.

We laid at anchor there for almost a week, and during that time I had my seventeenth birthday. I received no birthday cards, and certainly no birthday cake. Still, my consolation, I suppose, was that we were all alive and well.

Strangely enough I believe that after my crossing of the temporary gangway, enabling the others to follow, my shipmates seemed more kindly disposed towards me. At least I only got the odd clout now whereas before it was regularly. They don't suffer fools lightly at sea.

Soon afterwards a gang of Irish stevedores came out to the ship. They burned through the chains holding the deck cargo of timber which promptly fell into Lough Foyle. They then formed the timber into rafts and towed it into Londonderry. Freed from its weight the ship regained an even keel and we were taken into the port proper, where the rest of the cargo was checked for safety. All was well, because the next day two tugs arrived and we began the long tow to Troon in Scotland; uneventfully, I'm glad to say. There the rest of the cargo was to be unloaded and the old *Fidelio*'s damage assessed, probably in dry dock.

Once again I was summoned, along with my Irish pal, to the captain's quarters. Apparently there were now some Scandinavian seamen ashore and available to join their countrymen. So Paddy and I were to be paid off and sent to Glasgow at once to join a British ship. Old Captain Pedreaux shook hands, thanked us and wished us 'God Speed', and I swear the old hero had a lump in his throat; I know I did. Now we were headed for Glasgow and whatever the future might hold.

7

From a Tramp to a Castle

The first thing I did on arrival in Glasgow was to book a room at the Sailors' Home on the 'Broomilaw'. Around the corner was James Watt Street, where the Shipping Federation Offices were; it was there we had to report as soon as possible.

I didn't really want to hang around Glasgow for any length of time anyway, principally because I was almost broke. This was because after paying off from the *Fidelio* I'd had to stock myself up again with socks, underwear warmer clothing, etc. Fortunately seamen had extra clothing coupons, so it presented no problems in that respect. I also met another Irish lad who was roughly in the same boat as I was. He'd found out that we could get a decent meal at the Flying Angel canteen nearby, and also knew about another organisation committed to the welfare of seamen in general, where genuine applicants were given gifts of socks, jerseys and other items donated by kindly civilians. We had a great time that day. We had two slap-up meals, and managed to fill up our kit-bags with scarves, jerseys and socks, and got back to the Sailors' Home feeling pretty content.

The following morning we arrived at the shipping office to sign on for what was known as the 'pool'. This was a contract that meant we would be paid until we, or rather *they*, found a ship. As it happened we had no time to worry about having to hang around in Glasgow too long, for within the hour we'd been interviewed, accepted and given a train voucher to join a ship lying at anchor down the Clyde at Gourock, otherwise known as, 'The Tail of The Bank'.

As we made our way to St Enoch's station for the trip to Gourock we were part of a motley crowd; there were deck seamen, firemen, other engine-room personnel, stewards and more. On arrival we were embarked on an old fishing boat, which had been pressed into service as a ferry, and eventually came alongside the biggest ship I'd ever seen. This was to be my home for another year, and I was to have a far better eighteenth birthday aboard her than my seventeenth in Lough Foyle.

This then was the SS *Llanstephan Castle*, a ship belonging to the Union Castle Line whose pre-war trade was to South Africa with passengers and cargo. She was to continue in that capacity, but this time her passengers would be young soldiers and sailors – all seeming utterly bewildered at the turn of events that had seen them called up for war service and after only the most basic of training sent on their way to the other side of the world. The most poignant thing about them was the brave, nonchalant air they all assumed to hide their doubts. Most of them put on a show of bravado, as we all do when faced with something beyond our understanding and control. However, I think that deep down most of these lads knew that somehow their lives would never be the same again.

Still, here we all were, and before very long we were moving off to join our convoy and set sail for parts unknown.

On our first day at sea we were given our duties. I was made a bridge runner, which meant four hours on duty, followed by eight hours off. During my daylight watches I had to keep the bridge tidy and clean – and keep out of the captain's and officers' way. While on night duty I had to keep a lookout, and bring hot drinks and sandwiches to whoever was the officer of the watch. It was tedious, but off watch we passed our time by exploring the rest of the ship, which was enormous with seven decks.

We crossed the Bay of Biscay and soon the weather improved. Slowly we began to see land on the port side and found we'd arrived at Freetown in Sierra Leone. This had been turned into a convoy base, having as it did a large natural harbour. No sooner had we dropped anchor than a swarm of canoes were alongside selling local fruit and other items, in exchange for cigarettes. By the following day half of the crew and most of the soldiers had stomach upsets from the fruit, and were cursing the 'bum boat' natives, as they were known.

Soon we raised anchor and formed up into convoy formation again for the next leg of our voyage. It was now obvious that we were on our way to either India or the Middle East, via the Cape of Good Hope.

Suddenly, a few days later, there was frenzied activity on the deck, with dozens of soldiers erecting a makeshift canvas pool under the guidance of our bosun. It turned out that this was for the traditional ceremony of crossing the 'line' – as the equator is nicknamed in naval parlance. In this some member of the crew dresses up as Father Neptune and initiates all those who've never crossed the equator before. I think this must have been a real morale booster for all our passengers, who by this time were showing all the signs of dejection which cramped sleeping accommodation and three indifferent meals a day produced. I don't think anyone was to blame. It was simply that troops, and many of them, needed to be transported overseas, and the catering facilities were stretched to breaking point.

After leaving Freetown we seemed to be heading well out into the Atlantic, obviously to confuse Jerry as it was rumoured that a surface raider was prowling this area. However, at last we reached Table Bay, and were moored alongside in Cape Town, South Africa.

The view of the famous Table Mountain, that I'd only seen pictures of in books, was breathtaking, and as we crew members were given every afternoon off, some of us spent as much time taking in the scenery as possible. Despite my upbringing, which had instilled a highly developed awareness of 'man's inhumanity to man', I was still taken aback by the squalor that the poor native Africans lived in. Here was a country with a beautiful climate, and yet the people to whom it belonged had been dispossessed and were treated like subhumans. I walked the length of Adderly Street, the main thoroughfare of Cape Town, taking in all the sights and I don't think I saw more than two black people. And yet *they* were the rightful owners, or at least the inheritors, of this beautiful country.

Once again, as I'd seen in my early years, I was witnessing the ruthless greed of those in power, to whom everybody's life except their own was just a commodity to be used or cast aside at their whim. What a world . . ! When will it change, I wonder?

We finally left Cape Town, and our next stop was another

beautiful city, Durban in Natal, South Africa. We were to spend another week here taking on cargo and stores for the next part of our voyage.

Durban was a city of contrasts again. Lined up outside the docks were two-seater, rickshaw-like carriages. These were pulled by huge Zulu men, and except for an odd horse-drawn buggy were the only means of transport into the city centre. It was a novel experience and these rickshaw men were impressive. Once they'd got their passengers settled down, they balanced themselves between the shafts and set off. They quickly got into a stride, and to watch them running and chanting in their own tongue was a unique experience; they seemed to possess a dignity all their own.

The city centre was beautifully laid out, and West Street, the main street, was absolutely bustling. The main attraction was a cinema and entertainment centre called The Playhouse. If you looked up at the ceiling it was designed to resemble the night sky with stars twinkling, which was very eye-catching to say the least.

However, with my keen eye for detail I couldn't help noticing the absolute contrast between the life-styles of the indigenous people and the white people who were in control. The only redeeming feature of the poverty in South Africa was the fact that food, particularly fruit, was abundant, plentiful and cheap. Also, no one would suffer from chilblains in this climate.

At last our sojourn in Durban came to an end. As we sailed out of the harbour we had to pass a long finger of land on the starboard side of the bay known as the Bluff. High on the top of this promontory stood the 'Lady in White'. She'd apparently been a singer of some note in her day, and now every time a convoy left she would stand up there singing patriotic songs; *Land of Hope and Glory* etc., to the departing troops in a kindly attempt to boost morale. I saw her many times over the ensuing years and she never failed to bring a lump to many throats, including mine.

Now rumours were rife again, every one of which gave a different destination, but the main guess was Port Taufiq at the eastern end of the Suez Canal.

Those of us on board who were experienced sailors – well, I *had* by now done a year at sea – had taken note of where the sun rose and set to determine our course. But we might as well have used a crystal ball, because the convoy was zig-zagging as usual. One of my predictions was that we were heading for Antarctica, and I didn't think the war had reached there yet.

Then after all the rumour and speculation, our original theories were proved right, we did finally arrive at Port Taufiq in Egypt, and it was now obvious that our troops and cargo were destined for the Middle East.

Port Taufiq really doesn't merit a mention, except for the heat, flies and absolutely voracious street vendors who sold, or 'tried' to sell, a variety of shoddy souvenirs and crude pornographic material. Their method was to give the impression of great secrecy, only showing a glimpse of their wares. Anyone gullible enough to fall for the swindle would usually find, once the vendor had miraculously vanished, that they had an envelope of badly taken snaps of the Pyramids. Still, a fool and his money . . !

We were there about ten days discharging cargo. The troops had long gone and were now probably facing Rommel and his Africa Corps. But at last we sailed, and once again the conjecture started as to where we were headed this time. The same old guessing game.

Regardless of this, I'd like to say at this point that my choice of a seafaring role in the war suited me a treat. I visited places and met people who made an indelible impression on me which still remains sixty years later, and I wouldn't have missed a minute of it.

After the usual toing and froing, we joined another convoy and set sail once more. This voyage I remember not only for the fact that having no troops aboard we were like a ghost ship, but also because the ship's bo's'n – a nasty piece of work in my opinion – set us to cleaning decks and doing a thousand and one other jobs that had been neglected while carrying troops. We were at it from six in the morning until six in the evening, until thankfully after turning west into the setting sun we anchored in the harbour of Mombasa in Kenya, East Africa.

The next day we were allowed shore leave. The bo's'n disagreed with this, but the chief officer overruled his opinion. I don't think he liked the bo's'n anymore than we did. Having said this, I realise that the bo's'n was a very fine seaman, and was outstanding among a lot of other very good seamen, obviously he wouldn't have had his job if it had been otherwise. I must emphasise here that a merchant ship's crew are all chosen for their expertise in their 'particular' job. Anyone who isn't up to the task is given a bad discharge when a voyage ends, and would find it almost impossible to get another ship. My reasons for disliking this bo's'n were that he was all too aware of his own prowess, but treated the rest of us as though we were idiots. As I've said, I didn't like him, and as much as I was able to I kept out of his way.

Mombasa wasn't a patch on the South African cities I'd visited, but a hundred times better than Port Taufiq. The street market in Kilindini, its neighbouring town was astonishing, but strangely nearly all of the market traders were Indian. A lot of the stalls were displaying a myriad of spices, sauces and beautiful Indian chutneys, and we were exhorted to try this one and that one. Of course, they were clever salesmen and by the time I'd got to the end I had a bag full of different jars. Still, they were cheap and tasty and would perk up the Board of Trade set menu on board.

The British merchant service were fed a set menu for the twenty-one weekly meals, and no matter where you sailed to, or whatever the climate, it never varied. It was laid down by the Board of Trade in London and was strictly adhered to. Naturally some more enlightened stewards would vary things slightly, but overall you knew on Monday morning the menu that would obtain for the rest of the week. This obviously got a bit boring month in, month out, so the curries and spices would be a welcome addition to the menu.

We took on stores and cargo bound for Egypt again, and then the day before we sailed about a thousand black troops embarked, led by white officers. These were The Kings African Rifles regiment. They were destined for Egypt, and years later I found out that the future despot Idi Amin was among them. I think he was a corporal or sergeant. What a pity he survived to become the evil tyrant that he did. Think of the thousands of lives that would have been saved if only one little German bullet had found him. But they say the devil looks after his own, and only the good die young.

At last we were fully loaded and left Mombasa for Egypt again. Whether the authorities were getting confident or not I don't know, but we didn't join a convoy for the voyage north. Instead we had an escort of an old pre-war destroyer. I think we felt safer with this than if we'd been in convoy. She steamed around us like an old mother hen, and the reassuring sight of her guns and depth charges took a lot of the anxiety away. We all felt as though we were in good hands, and the trip north passed peacefully.

8

Christmas in the Indian Ocean

By this time Christmas was approaching, and it dawned on me that this would be the second one I'd spent away from home. Christmas had always been a happy time when we were growing up. There were never a lot of presents, obviously, but somehow Mam and Dad always managed miraculously to make the festive season happy. This was long before the Christmas tree became popular, so Mam would tie two barrel hoops together and hang a few half-penny baubles on them, after first wrapping them with tissue paper. This was known as a Christmas bush. It was hung from the ceiling in the centre of the room, then streamers made from more tissue paper were draped around the room. The whole effect to us lads was magical. I've often thought that with the gas light and paraffin lamp as our only illumination, these actually seemed to enhance the effect. Bill, my older brother, and I were junior entrepreneurs before the term became widespread. As a matter of fact most of the lads in Barrow, and probably elsewhere, could earn a few pence honestly (sometimes not 'quite so'), and in those days it all went into the home kitty.

All these thoughts went through my head as we steamed north, and I wondered how Jim, my younger brother, and the two lassies Sheila and Gladys, my younger sisters, were. My memory went back to those happy days, and I thought of Mam without her family, and Dad with his false legs having to trudge about in the blackout, and I'm afraid it was all too much and I was overcome with grief. I sat on my bunk and broke my heart. I didn't feel like a tough man of the sea then at all, just a seventeen-year-old boy

c

who was very homesick for a little place called Hindpool. Thankfully the mood passed eventually, and before long we were preparing for port.

We arrived at Port Taufiq the next day, and luckily there was no time to dwell on personal problems. It took about a week to discharge our cargo and the black soldiers. Then there were three busy days of deck scrubbing, until Simon Legree, the task master bo's'n was satisfied. Not that he said as much, but we took his grunts to be as far as he would go towards saying thank you.

Next we started to load more equipment and troops, and the rumour this time was that we were going to India. For a second time the rumours turned out to be true. But this time the troops were a different crowd altogether. They'd all seen action in the deserts of North Africa, and had a look of what I can only describe as patient resignation. They knew that they had a job to do, and unpleasant and dangerous as it was they wouldn't shirk it.

Finally everything was ready and we were to join two other ships and two destroyer escorts for the voyage to India. So once again it was down the Red Sea, through the Gulf of Aden and out into the Indian Ocean. By this time it was the 22nd of December 1940, and apart from everything else we were all, crew and soldiers alike, full of what Christmas meant to each of us in his own way.

Of course, us seamen were all still fully occupied doing our watches etc., and all the usual shipboard chores. But once again my deeply ingrained sense of what social justice should be, had me thinking of these army lads, most of whom had selflessly volunteered, though some were conscripts, and all stoically going wherever they were sent. Of course they had their little grumbles, that is our British tradition, but nevertheless they were going to fight an enemy not of their choosing, in deserts and jungles thousands of miles from all they loved and held dear.

Since then I've often thought of the utter hypocrisy of the rotten political mountebanks in Britain and Europe who for one reason or another had allowed all this to happen. I don't believe all the historian's clap-trap about Adolf Hitler's inevitable rise to power. He could, and should have been stopped when he first started spouting his evil bile. But of course there were elements who silently, and some not so silently, applauded all he did. He was the bulwark against the Russian Bear, and the grim spectre of communism as they saw it. And so they helped to create a bigger monster who as we all know became uncontrollable. Consequently the world suffered. Untold millions died needlessly, millions more were crippled both physically and mentally before the carnage was ended and the madman took his own life in Berlin

Christmas Day dawned and there seemed to be a feeling of comradeship in the air with the troops who were our passengers entering into the Christmas spirit. Lads who'd never spoken to each other before shook hands and wished each other a Happy Christmas and a better New Year. Festivity-wise I think our ship's catering staff did a marvellous job of producing a really good Christmas dinner, complete with traditional pudding and white sauce. Even the troops complimented them. It was a great day under the circumstances.

I went on watch on the bridge at eight o'clock, and had the shock of my life to see the ship's master, Captain Cove, standing there wishing everyone the compliments of the season – even me. Normally he wouldn't have noticed that I existed. We were treated as the lowest form of life by the senior officers as a rule, so this proved that after all, in certain circumstances, they could act like human beings . . . Christmas should come more often.

So on we sailed until we finally reached Bombay in India, and once again I came face to face with a vastly different culture to anything I'd ever seen before, or even imagined. India was breathtaking. We were piloted to the Alexander Dock where our troops were disembarked, and we started to unload our cargo, as well as restocking our own supplies ready for whatever the powers that be had in mind for us next.

I think we were in Bombay for almost a week, during which time two or three of us would hire a 'gharry', which was a horse-drawn carriage, and cheap by any standards, for a day. We visited most of the places of interest, and once again I was astonished at the sight of great wealth existing alongside absolutely dire poverty. I think at that time life expectancy in the subcontinent was about thirty years. I saw entire families who spent their whole lives living on the pavements under the most flimsy shelters imaginable. Begging seemed to be their only source of income and it was pitiful to see them bowing and scraping over a gift of a few annas, though to them I suppose it was the difference between a little food or none. I decline further comment on this, because anyone who knows me will already know my feelings about it.

Towards the end of our stay in India I was sent by the bo's'n one day to check all the wooden wedges that we used to secure the canvas covers to the hatch tops. To my surprise I found a group of Indian dock workers breaking open cases of canned beef and hiding the tins in their clothing. They were petrified with fear at my arrival, thinking I would report them. I quickly calmed them down and helped them to open another case before showing them the best way to get ashore without being discovered. What they made of me I don't know. To them I represented authority, I suppose. How were they to know that authority was anathema to me, and that I would have bitten my tongue out rather than report them for stealing food.

So finally we sailed again for another unknown destination, though by this time we were becoming more adept at recognising different signs that indicated possible directions. We'd taken quite a varied cargo on board, also approximately five hundred passengers. These varied from soldiers being sent home through illness, to a lot of families of what appeared to be civil service people being repatriated, and three hundred Gurkha soldiers. These Gurkhas were fascinating little men who sat on deck in the sunshine endlessly sharpening their huge curve-bladed knives called kukris. Apparently they only drew these knives in an emergency, and if it was drawn at any other time they had to draw blood with it. Some of the crew were foolish enough to ask these little warriors if they could see their kukris, and were taken aback when asked to hold out a hand to be nicked so that blood appeared. After a while no one else was daft enough to ask.

We plodded across the Indian Ocean, not actually in convoy, but with two other ships and a destroyer escort. We landed back in Durban some time in February 1941, and for a change there was some mail from home. This once again brought a lump to my throat, and made me realise how much I missed home and family. I wished our next voyage would be to the UK.

It was about this time that some South African families formed an association to invite merchant seamen to their homes for a well deserved break away from ship life. I was invited by a family called McPhail, the husband was a manager of some sort on the

South African Railways. He was of Scottish ancestry and they were a kindly family. I had a great time at their home and after a magnificent lunch (to me it was dinner) we motored up into the Valley of a Thousand Hills. The scenery was wonderful and I enjoyed their company and the day out as well. The only fly in the ointment, and it put me off going again, was the way they treated their black staff. They had two large Mastiff type dogs, and as far as I could see the dogs were treated better than the black human beings. Naturally after all their kindness I couldn't say anything about this, but although there was an invitation to visit them any time I was in Durban, I never went again.

After almost two weeks we were loaded with cargo again and had embarked about twelve hundred troops. A lot of them were white South African lads, and once again I was struck by the cultural divide. Their equipment was far superior to anything the British lads had. They also possessed an attitude of superiority which I found offensive. Still, they were on our side, and even though every time any of us crew were within earshot they lapsed into Afrikaans, I suppose this was reasonable since it was their native language. Forty short years before, their grandads and possibly their fathers had fought bravely against the British in the Boer War.

I was going on duty one night when I heard one of the most poignant sounds I had ever heard, it was a couple of hundred of these South African soldiers singing the old Afrikaan's song, *Sari Marais*, and my heart went out to them. Any animosity I felt towards them evaporated immediately. I realised then that just the same as our troops, a lot of them were going to die or be wounded in the common fight against the German enemy, and felt they should be praised in spite of any superficial attitudes.

By now we were on our way north to the Red Sea and Egypt again. I think that about this time, as the war seemed to be spreading from Europe to the Middle and Far East, people had long began to realise that the initial attitude of, 'It'll all be over by Christmas', was a delusion. We were in for a long, hard struggle before the lights would come on again.

So we were in Egypt again. All the troops and cargo were discharged, and the uncertainty of 'where to next?' came up for debate once more. This turned out to be Mombasa in Kenya again. But first we had to call in at Point Docks in Durban to load a cargo of munitions for the North African campaign, which at that time wasn't going too well for the allies. On arrival in Mombasa we embarked more troops and transported the whole lot up north to Egypt.

9

Reunion in Bombay

This toing and froing was becoming tiresome and tempers were getting frayed. Fights broke out among the crew over trivialities that normally would have been laughed off. Even the officers were on edge and I got many a telling off that I thought was unfair. In the middle of April we set off once more for Bombay, and again I thought of Bill's birthday and wondered where he was doing his bit. He was probably just as fed up as I was.

I think the captain, a very wise old 'Cove' (as already mentioned his name actually was Cove – but no pun intended) saw the tensions on board mounting, and upon arrival in India half of the crew were given three days off all duties, and encouraged to go ashore for a complete change. It was a marvellous break, and I think it came just in the nick of time. I was lucky enough to be in the first half to be given leave, and off two or three of us went to make the most of it together.

Coming back to the ship after the first day ashore I was stopped at the foot of the gangway by two Indians. They presented me with a little parcel, and smiling at me gave the impression that they wanted me to open it. Until then I hadn't recognised them, but it now dawned on me that they were two of the dock workers who I'd helped to steal the tins of corned beef on the previous trip to Bombay. The present was a beautiful little fifty-year calendar in Indian brassware. I was pretty overwhelmed by this and immediately earmarked it as a present for my mother . . . She actually treasured it all her life, but I daren't ever tell her the real story behind her gift. She'd probably have walloped me for encouraging theft. However, I knew personally that I'd done the right thing – redistributing wealth to someone in need.

We left India in the first week of May 1941. Once more we had a passenger list composed of men, women and children. This time, however, they were the owners, managers and their families from the tea plantations of Assam and elsewhere. Apparently, because of the speed of the Japanese advance it had been deemed better to repatriate them home for safety.

On or about the 10th of May, I had the sad experience of my first burial at sea. A little girl of about six had died of some tropical illness. We assembled on the after deck for a church service conducted by the chief officer. Then the tiny canvas-wrapped body was committed to the deep. We hadn't known her of course, but we still shared the family's sorrow at such a tragedy. Today the little mite would have been brought home for a burial in familiar surroundings, but those were not normal times.

On the 13th of May I was eighteen. I thought, here we go again, not a single card, it's going to be as dismal as my seventeenth. I was so wrong. At noon I went along to the crew's mess room and about twenty of my younger shipmates gave a noisy, but sincere rendition of, *Happy Birthday to You*. One of the cooks had baked a passable cake, and I even got some small gifts and home-made cards from pals. It was great.

I was in my cabin reading that same afternoon when one of the junior officers came along to the door. He asked my name and then asked if it was my birthday. When I said it was, he told me to get dressed as though I was going ashore and to be in the first class passenger dining-room at three-thirty, and not to be a minute late. At first I thought it was a hoax, but then realised that an officer would not be a party to that.

I was on time and I found a birthday party in progress to which I'd been invited. It was for a little eight-year-old girl and we were both introduced. Her name was Diane Phelps, and I've often been tempted to try and find her, if only to return the little printed 'menu' of the occasion I still have. The party ended a lovely day, and I felt at peace with the world that night.

The following day the ship was alive with rumours which thankfully turned out to be true. We were to call at Durban and

Cape Town, then join a convoy for Blighty (the UK) and home.

We stayed at Durban for three days where some more civilian and army personnel joined us, then it was on to Cape Town. When we arrived there the quayside where we tied up resembled an armed camp. There were soldiers and police everywhere. Under their eagle-eyed supervision lines of dock workers carried small boxes aboard and into a special hold known as the 'Specie Room', which was in effect a massive safe.

We were only in Cape Town for thirty-six hours before sailing out to join our convoy bound for home. It was not until later that I found out the reason for all that security. Those boxes contained a huge fortune in gold bullion. Why anyone with half a brain would think the gold would be safer in the UK at that time of the war was beyond my comprehension. Still, ours not to reason why . . .

We left Cape Town and had no sooner cleared Table Bay when we hit one of the most violent storms our experienced crew members had ever sailed in. The commodore ship of the convoy, was a large Polish vessel named the *Batory*. Pre-war she'd been one of the proud fleet of Gydinia America Lines, and fortunately she'd been out on the North Atlantic passenger run when Poland was over-run, thus keeping her out of German hands. She hoisted a flag signal which when deciphered meant, roughly, that it was 'every ship for herself until the weather abated'. By this time my ship was rolling at least thirty degrees, first to port and then to starboard. At first I was terrified. I thought, the next roll will be her last. When she reached the extreme of her roll she seemed to hover there for seconds and I thought, she'll never recover. But gradually she did and then she'd go through the whole gut-wrenching procedure the other way. I think the wind was the most frightening aspect of it all. It was gusting at over a hundred miles an hour, sending sea spray right over the top of the bridge.

By this time Captain Cove, our skipper, decided enough was enough. I was out on the wing of the bridge on lookout duty and clinging on like grim death – we daren't put our heads above the canvas 'dodgers' designed to turn the wind up and away from us. He first rang down to the engine-room and told them his intentions, next he sent runners round to tell everyone else to hang on to anything substantial. He was waiting for a tiny lull in the wind – I swore later that he could actually 'see' the wind – and after interminable minutes which seemed an age, he almost gave the helmsman a heart attack with a screamed, "HARD TO PORT . . !" The old girl responded almost at once. She listed dangerously over to port as a great gust struck her starboard side like a blow from a giant fist. But Captain Cove, 'Master Mariner', and a twenty-five year old ship, between them saved all our lives that day as she came round. We were now sailing due south with the storm behind us.

All through the night we kept on south, and at daybreak the following day we'd left the worst behind us. Another 180 degree turn put us back on our true course, and now we had to find the convoy and resume our homeward bound journey. Hopefully the next port of call would be Freetown in Sierra Leone, West Africa; known then as 'the white man's grave'.

I'd like to say a word or two here about our skipper, and all the other brave skippers of merchant ships. The British examinations to pass first the second mate's ticket, followed by the mate's or chief officer's ticket, and finally the master's or captain's ticket are the most difficult qualifications to acquire of any merchant navy in the world. Later on in my years at sea I studied hard myself to sit for the second mate's ticket, but the sheer scale of knowledge required beat me, and frankly I gave up. The result of these most stringent of hurdles is that Britain has, alongside the Scandinavians, the finest qualified officers in the world. Whenever a ship flew the Red Ensign, or the 'Red Duster' as we affectionately called it, you could be certain that her captain, officers and crew were first class seamen, for all their human frailties. What a pity the nation never fully appreciated them. Another satisfying fact is that ninety-nine per cent of these men never even saw a public school. They came up from the fo'c'sle, and clawed their way to the top on merit alone.

It took us almost a week to reach Freetown, and as we sailed north we met up with other ships of the convoy who had been forced to scatter the same as we had. Between us we formed ranks and achieved some sort of protection amongst ourselves. Our escorts had fled, and who could blame them in such atrocious weather. Some of the crews on these small escort vessels spent their lives wet through, and in mortal danger whenever the weather turned bad; and had no hot meals for weeks on end. They deserved a medal for the life-style they had to put up with.

We reached Freetown at last, and before the anchor had been dropped the native 'bum boats' were swarming around us, attempting to barter their half-ripe fruit, or diving for coins thrown by the crew and passengers. They were persistent if nothing else.

Personally I had no interest in these goings on for the simple reason that I had blinding, painful toothache. I'd reported to the sick-bay nurse, and was sitting on my bunk commiserating with myself when a bridge runner (messenger) came and told me to go at once to the ship's sick bay. The nurse in charge told me I was to go ashore in a launch with one of the passengers, who was also suffering from toothache. I was in too much pain to have any misgivings and so away we went. The dentist's surgery was on the second floor of the Grand Hotel. And if any place was misnamed that hotel was, it was anything but grand.

The dentist was a huge black man, and his nurse/assistant was also quite large. I was given a cold drink and sent out onto a veranda while he dealt with the passenger. I'd never seen such primitive equipment in a dentist's surgery, it was pre-war, but certainly not this war. The dentist then brought me in for treatment. He was a very taciturn individual who didn't waste words where a grunt would suffice. The nurse behind the chair brought my head back and put her arm across my forehead. Then the dentist opened my mouth and peered in. He didn't waste time on extras such as cocaine or any other deadening agent, and before I had time to worry, with a dexterity obviously gained from practice, he extracted four of my teeth in seconds. The instant relief from what must have been a large abscess over-rode any pain I had from losing my teeth. I mumbled my thanks to him, then the passenger and I were ferried back to the ship, to recover and dwell on dentistry 'African style'. Primitive, but very effective.

So once again the commodore ship, *Batory*, went to the head of the convoy, and the rest of us were instructed by flag signals, and Aldis lamp messages in morse code, where to take our positions. The convoy was led by a cruiser in front of the *Batory*, and there were also four destroyers on the outside of our four lanes of merchant men. My ship, the *Llanstephan Castle*, was right in the centre of them all. Standing out on the wing of the bridge one night I overheard the second mate telling someone in the wheel-house that we had prime position because of all the South African Gold we were carrying. This cheered me up no end, and being only human I couldn't wait to pass on this nugget of news (no pun intended) to my shipmates, and I think it bucked them all up.

So at long last we were on our way back to Britain. All that lay between us was about four-thousand miles of ocean, a distance which by the time we'd zig-zagged across it would be almost doubled. Still, we were heading in the right direction, and I think the air of excitement that now permeated the ship affected everyone on board. Some of the Indian service people who were being repatriated had been away from home for as much as seven or eight years.

Travel was by much slower systems in those days, and all overseas travel was by ship. British Imperial Airways had introduced Flying Boats before the war. These were huge aircraft which took off and landed on water, and were at that time the last word in luxury travel, but only affordable by the 'intrepid' rich.

By now we were well out into the Atlantic and changing course frequently, but at least we were evading Jerry. The monotony of going on watch and then back again to your bunk began to get on our nerves, so you can imagine the feeling of euphoria when a destroyer came out from Scotland to meet us, and our escorts who'd shepherded us home took off with a hoot of their whistles, and an answering blast of gratitude from all the rest of the convoy.

10

Dear Old Glasgow Again

We had reached the mouth of the Clyde, and my ship was being piloted up river to York Hill Docks to discharge passengers and cargo. We would then be signed off and find out what leave we'd be allowed. As far as I was concerned it was next stop Barrow-in-Furness and 'home'.

The quayside was like an armed camp again, and once the ship was moored and a gangway placed in position, dozens of soldiers came aboard and began carrying the gold bullion ashore. Until they'd finished no one was allowed ashore. It didn't take long and once the bullion had been driven away things returned to normal.

That evening we had to queue at the second officer's cabin to draw an advance of wages to enable us to go ashore that night if we wished; without a doubt we did. We were also told that if we wanted to re-sign on the ship we would only be given four days of leave, because the ship was due to leave Glasgow once she was cleared of cargo. I declined to re-sign on as I definitely wanted more than four days at home, so I was told to report to the Glasgow shipping office ten days hence when I would be given another ship. This suited me much better as it meant I'd then have a decent length of time at home.

Three of us decided to spend that night exploring Glasgow, so off we went all dressed up. Eventually we found ourselves in Argyll Street near the Central Station, where I was startled to hear a voice shouting across the road, "Jervla deksgut," in Norwegian, which roughly translated meant 'bloody deck boy' – I think. When the shouters crossed over the road I was delighted to see that it was Big Nils and another seaman, Eric Fivelsdal from my last ship the *Fidelio*. They seemed pleased to see me again and we exchanged stories about our present ships. During this chat Big Nils told me that when the *Fidelio* had been dry-docked it had been decided that the damage under her rudder and propeller could only have been caused by our running over a U-boat. This obviously pleased Nils, because he had guessed it at the time. So perhaps we had sunk a U-boat after all; though we would never know.

We shook hands and parted, so pleased to have met once more. I wished them well and felt vindicated, because I'd told this story to my present shipmates and they'd all scoffed at me. I was able to scoff back now that Nils had substantiated it for me.

So it was back on board the *Llanstephan Castle* for what I thought would be my last night's sleep aboard her, but once again fate was to prove me wrong. I was so excited thinking about home, my mother and father, Sheila, Gladys and young Jim, I don't think I closed my eyes all that night. I could see them all in my thoughts. I also wondered where Bill was, and wondered if he might even have been shipped overseas. Possibly on one of the ships in the convoy we took out without my knowing. Still, I should know tomorrow.

The next morning we were ushered into an empty first class dining-room where we were signed off, given our balance of wages and a return travel warrant to Barrow. I felt like a king. I had almost seventy pounds in my pocket and I was going home. I felt as if I was walking on air.

Four of us booked a taxi and set off for Glasgow Central. I would change at Carnforth to catch the Barrow train, while the other lads were going on further south. I think the effect of the sleepless night was telling on me because I dozed off and slept all the way to Carnforth.

I hadn't long to wait for a train and at last we pulled into Barrow station. This was to be my first shock. It had been badly bombed and I immediately recalled my dad's words that innocent civilians would suffer as much in this war as the fighting men. Here was the evidence. I set off for Hindpool and passed more of Jerry's handiwork on the way. I was dying to reach home and yet dreading what I might find. Hindpool turned out to have had more than its share of bombs, but the Scotch Buildings were intact.

Sadly my family were not.

Mam greeted me at the door and she looked ill. We clung to each other and I felt an utter, and overwhelming feeling of sadness to think that I had been the cause of some of her misery. But when you're eighteen consideration for the unhappiness of someone else is a fleeting emotion, and I wanted to see her smile.

I discovered that Jim, my younger brother, had also run away to sea like myself, and into the bargain had chosen a Norwegian tanker, the SS *Morgenen*. I don't know how long he'd sailed on her, but he was now home and waiting to join the Royal Navy. The two lassies, little Sheila and Gladys were away, having been evacuated to somewhere in Westmorland – now part of Cumbria. Brother Bill had apparently married a girl in London, and so naturally spent all his leaves there with his wife. However, the most heartbreaking news of all, was that Dad had left us all and was living with another woman.

I don't think that in all the sixty years since then I've seen a woman so drained and forlorn as my mother was that day. What made it all the more cruel was the fact that for all her married life she had been the rock we'd all clung to, father included. I was hurt and angry and certainly bitter that he could inflict this kind of misery on someone who had worshipped him all her life.

I swore that day that I would never speak to him again. And although over the years I've had painful regrets, and thought that perhaps if I'd been a little older and wiser I might have behaved differently, I've stuck to my promise. This is a memory that if it were possible I'd try to forget, but on that day I felt that the only course open to me was the one I took. I felt then, and I still do, that at that moment what my mother needed was reassurance. I gave her my total loyalty, and because of this I'm sure that day was a turning point for her. I think Jim went and tried to talk my father into a reconciliation, but to no avail. That chapter in our lives was ended. As I've said I never spoke to him again, and I'm sure we both lost a great deal of happiness over the years because of this.

I knew I had to get Mam away from that scene of misery, so the following day I proposed that we went to see the lassies. She agreed, so off we went to Penrith. Once there we hired a taxi and spent some lovely hours with two little lassies who, on the surface at least, were making the most of what at their ages must have been a great wrench at leaving their home in Barrow. The fact that there were thousands of other kids in the same position was no consolation at all.

We came home and I proposed another trip at the end of the week. This delighted Mam, so at last, in spite of the upheaval, a little colour was back in her face, and some of her wonderful spirit was returning. The day of our next trip came, but on this visit after seeing the girls off to school then getting ready for home Mam took ill. I was to return to Glasgow the following day to join my next ship, so we were in a quandary. I had to get back to Barrow and pack my kit-bag ready for the journey. Fortunately our dilemma was solved by one of the lasses' 'hostesses'; she said she would put Mam to bed and look after her until she was well enough to go home. I think her name was Braithwaite, we were very grateful for her kindness, and I knew Mam would be in good hands.

So for me it was back to Barrow, where I think Jim and I got blotto on a pub crawl. All in all I'd had a leave to remember, and I hoped it wouldn't be as long before my next home visit. I think I'd come to realise even more how dear my family was to me, but I'm too undemonstrative to have shown it.

Next day I said my farewells and took the train to Glasgow. Young Jim was now on his way to service in the Royal Navy. So, with Bill in the army, all three of us were doing our bit for King and Country. I knew that we had a King, but I was a bit dubious about the Country. Up to that time the only evidence I had about it was what I'd been told.

11

Finding Relatives in Glasgow

I arrived in Glasgow and walked to the Broomilaw where I booked a cubicle at the Sailors' Home. Next day I would sign on and see what ships were looking for crews, and hopefully I would get a berth quite soon.

It was a lovely August evening, and when I'd had a meal I decided to try and find some relatives I had in Glasgow whom I had never met. When Mam had learned that I'd just come from Glasgow, and was about to return there, she'd given me some addresses and said I might look them up if I had time, so here was my chance.

The first address was in Kinmount Avenue (I can't recall the number) in a district called Cathcart. My instructions were to take a Mount Florida tram and ask the conductor where to get off. I found the house with no trouble, and feeling rather sheepish I knocked on the door. There was no answer, so I knocked a bit louder, but still got no answer. I began to wonder if I'd got the right house when an old lady in the house next door came out and asked me who I wanted. I told her that I'd come to look for my cousin Jenny Noble who I believed lived there with people called Hosey. I also told her that I was a merchant seaman and that I was in Glasgow to join a ship. At this her defensive attitude changed and she became quite solicitous; fortunately I didn't look like a thug or burglar, I hope. She said that the family were out on some sort of war effort, then asked me what I would do for the evening now that I was at a loose end. The truth was I didn't know, so she invited me into her home and I had the best high tea I'd had for a long time.

After tea she said she was taking her little dog for its evening walk, and if I cared I could go with her. We set off and must have walked miles. I saw the famous Hampden Park football stadium and enjoyed the old lady's company immensely. She then showed me where to get the tram back to the Sailors' Home, and having thanked her off I went.

The following day I presented myself at the shipping office. I hung around until lunch-time, but to no avail. Mr Hannah, who was the man to whom we had to report, made us sign the register and said we could have the rest of the day off.

Now was my chance to see if I could meet my cousin Jenny. I knew the routine now and soon found myself in Cathcart. I knocked and this time I was greeted with real enthusiasm. It appeared the old lady who'd befriended me the day before had told Mrs Hosey that I'd called. I spent a really nice afternoon and evening with them, and had a lovely chat with Jenny about her home in Bradford and mine in Barrow. What cousin Jenny was doing living at the Hosey's house in Glasgow I never knew. They seemed a bit reticent about it so I didn't ask, but I returned to Broomilaw as pleased as punch that I'd eventually met them all. I promised to keep in touch, but as so often happens unfortunately I didn't, and I've always regretted not doing so.

The following morning it was back to the shipping office. Here Mr Hannah took my name, and along with two or three other lads of about my age sent me into a back room for an interview with an elderly chap; who later turned out to be an ex-captain retired, and the 'crew examiner'.

When it was my turn I was given a list of questions to answer regarding seamanship, which I found quite easy. The old chap then asked me more questions. After this we were all sent back into the main room to await the results of the tests. Eventually Mr Hannah called me to the desk to inform me that I'd been promoted to 'sailor' rank, or almost an able-seaman. This was three years before I should have been. But before I had chance to get carried away with pride, Mr Hannah assured me that this was simply a stop-gap of expediency because of the horrendous loss of men and shipping at that time. This took the wind out of my sails a bit, but I realised that he only said it from a desire to stop my head swelling.

Along with about thirty other seamen we were taken by bus to a place called Inveraray on Loch Fyne; the castle home of the Dukes of Argyll. Here we were to join the MV *Winchester Castle*, another ship of the Union Castle Steamship Company, like my last ship.

The *Winchester* was a different and decidedly better vessel than the *Llanstephan;* altogether much larger and more up to date in every respect. Once again I was overawed by the sheer size of her, and to be quite honest at that moment I couldn't have been prouder to be an able seaman at eighteen years old, even though it was only through luck and expediency.

That journey by bus deserves a mention to show how far things have advanced since those days. At one point on the way to Inveraray we came to a long, steep hill known as the 'Rest and be Thankful'. The decrepit old bus stopped at the bottom, and we all had to get out and walk to the top because it couldn't climb up it carrying both us and our luggage. Luckily there was a pub at the top where we were able to get refreshments . . . amusing to look back on, but not very funny at the time.

However, having eventually arrived at Loch Fyne we were ferried out to the *Winchester Castle* aboard an old drifter and met at the top of the companionway by representatives of the ship's deck, engine-room, and catering departments. My crowd were taken to our quarters in the fo'c'sle where I was put in a long, narrow cabin with twelve bunks crammed into it. It wasn't exactly roomy, and I was to find out later that one of the bulkheads (walls) was also the bulkhead of the 'chain locker'. This was a large compartment that housed all the anchor chain, and believe me when the anchor was dropped the clatter of the huge chain running out was deafening. Still, there was nothing to be done about that, so we'd have to make the most of it.

As is usual when a crowd of strange men are together, friendships are formed and likes and dislikes aired until eventually an acceptable, amiable kind of relationship develops that allows quite different personalities to exist side by side without the usual frictions and fall-outs. I do also think that our generation were a deal more tolerant in such situations than the present one would be. Whether they would endure the conditions that obtained on a British merchant ship, or the primitive conditions soldiers and sailors had to put up with, is debatable.

67

However, hopefully we'll never have to find out. Of course, in those days we'd never had much in the way of material comforts, so probably our expectations were lower than today.

As the weeks rolled by we seemed to be involved in some kind of secret manoeuvres. We would take on board four or five hundred soldiers of the newly formed commando units, though at that time, October 1941, they were all just 'soldiers' to us. Exactly when they became known as Marine Commandos I've no idea, but the one group I vividly remember was the Fifth Commando, who would eventually be with us on the first successful invasion of enemy territory – but more of that later.

We always seemed to sail out during the night, but never very far, simply to the nearest isolated loch where our actions wouldn't be overseen. Apparently the whole purpose of our forays was to land our commando lads in some remote spot so as to improve their toughness and resilience by having to find their way to a given rendezvous in a certain length of time. One of the favourite landing places was in Loch Scridain on the south of the Island of Mull. The lads would then have to traverse the length of the Island and meet us in Tobermory. Inevitably there always seemed to be casualties; their treks must have been gruelling experiences. However, despite the fact that when the landing craft brought them back aboard they always looked bedraggled and weary, we never lost a single one of our lads.

While they were trekking overland we, of course, would sail around the Firth of Lorne into the Sound of Mull in comfort, and anchor off Tobermory to await their return. Looking back it must have been a nightmare for the navigation team taking such a large ship through these confined waters. Nevertheless we did it numerous times with no mishaps, luckily. A testimony to their skill.

One of my memories of anchoring off Tobermory still amuses me to this day, and I think it deserves a mention. We were given evening shore leave on one trip and decided to try the local brew. My pal at this time was a lad named Hendricks, his parents or grandparents were Dutch; although he had been born in London he spoke Dutch fluently; which impressed me immensely.

There was quite a crowd going ashore on the liberty boat, and upon landing Hendricks and I made for the hotel. One of the Royal Navy seamen who manned our landing craft called to me, "Don't go to the hotel, that's for officers only." It appeared there was another pub we were allowed to go to which was used by the locals. This made my hackles rise. Here we were in the middle of a war and class distinction still existed in a backwater like this. However, we were in effect civilians, so we marched straight into the hotel and ordered two pints. The barman didn't know what to make of us, but served us nevertheless. We took our pints and sat down in two of the most comfortable chairs, taking great satisfaction at the discomfiture of those around us. If looks could have killed, the glances of the second lieutenants there would have done so. A real officer would have taken it all in his stride, but that isn't the way with upstarts. Whether it was of any significance or not I don't know, but we were never allowed ashore in Tobermory again. I suspect, however, that the 'old boy's network' had worked again to put the lower orders in their place.

At this time, early December 1941, we were all thinking about Christmas, mainly as to whether we would get any home leave. This was the topic of most conversations until the news came of the perfidious Japanese attack on the American fleet at Pearl Harbour during the 7th & 8th of December. Most of us had never even heard of Pearl Harbour, and at that time any news we were given was heavily censored. It wasn't until many weeks later that we learned the true extent of the devastation the Japs had inflicted. They say that all's fair in love and war, but there are some things that are beyond the acceptable, and Pearl Harbour was one of these acts. In one fell swoop the American fleet had been decimated. I've often thought that for the Japanese it turned out to be a hollow victory, for the simple reason that although it had an immediate effect on American fighting capabilities in the Pacific, it filled the American people and their president with such determination to avenge it, that from that moment on the Japanese defeat was inevitable; even though this was only achieved after an appalling loss of life on both sides.

I gathered, listening to the feelings expressed by the older crew members at that time – a lot of whom had served in the First World War – that the Americans would be extremely welcome as allies, because until that moment Britain had stood almost alone, and events had been looking anything but rosy.

Still, it was almost Christmas and we were all wondering about who was being granted leave. The chief officer came up with a scheme that seemed fair; each cabin of deck personnel had twelve seamen, so each cabin put six blank and six marked pieces of paper in a hat and simply drew lots. Needless to say I drew a blank, so once again I'd have to spend Christmas away from home and I wasn't looking forward to the festive season one bit.

By this time we'd finished our latest operation and were anchored again in Loch Fyne. Our troops had all disembarked, and apart from about fifty naval personnel who'd manned the landing craft during the exercises we were like a ghost ship.

An air of despondency settled on us all as the bo's'n allocated watch duties to those of us who were left. I was to keep anchor watch on the bow of the ship to ensure that certain landmarks ashore remained constant. In other words to make sure the ship didn't drag her anchor. In actual fact this would have been very unlikely as there was no wind, and the surface of Loch Fyne was like a mill pond. Still, ours not to reason why, and at least it helped to pass the time.

Christmas Day dawned and as the day wore on we were fortified by a really good Christmas dinner (at midday) so our spirits gradually rose. We were all given four cans of beer as a present from the ship, and as I was on anchor watch at 4pm I decided to drink mine later. We were then pleasantly surprised by the arrival of the bo's'n and second officer at the door of our quarters. They both wished us all the season's greetings and told us that our watch would be given forty-eight hours shore leave as from midnight. This was an unexpected treat which meant that after I'd finished my anchor watch at 8pm I was free for Boxing Day and the day after. We could have two nights ashore without having to worry about going on watch early the next morning. So what had started out as a poor Christmas Day ended as a really pleasant one; though it was still not like going home.

I hope anyone reading these memories of mine will forgive me if I wander off at times, but my early years at sea were such a completely different life-style to anything I'd experienced before that I want the reader to feel some of the profound effect these changes had on me. If my little diversions convey that effect then I'll feel they've done the trick.

On Boxing Day three or four of us decided to go ashore and pass a few hours anywhere other than on board the ship. Previously I had found a little shop in Inveraray that mailed orders for the famous Harris Tweed cloth to anywhere in the

United Kingdom. In one of my letters home I'd mentioned this to Mam and sent her one of the sample books for her to choose from – or at least the shop owner had – so all I had to do now was go in and pay for what she'd picked and it would be dispatched. She'd chosen a really nice pattern, which she later had made up into a costume, and while I was in the shop I asked the owner if he'd had a nice Christmas. I was astonished to find that in Scotland they didn't have Christmas as a celebration at all. I thought of all the sparkle and happiness that Christmas meant to me, and felt sorry for them – they obviously didn't know what they were missing.

After I'd paid for the tweed I couldn't face the atmosphere of the Inveraray local pub and caught the next ferry back aboard ship. I couldn't inflict my dismal mood on my mates ashore and thought, 'I'm better on my own'. It had suddenly come home to me just how far-flung our family now was, and I wondered what sort of Christmas Mam was having almost alone. Dad was gone for good and Bill and I were miles away, our two little sisters were out in the wilds of Westmorland, and I knew that Jim was waiting to hear from the Royal Navy. I only hoped that he was still there to give her a little moral support. It completely took the gilt off my gingerbread that night and I went to my bunk a sad and miserable sailor.

Luckily a new day gives you a new perspective, and I spent the rest of my two days off getting my things ready for my ten days of leave when the first crowd returned.

The days passed, and soon on the second of January 1942, after a somewhat inebriated Hogmanay, both ashore and on board, those of us who were entitled to leave were given our travel vouchers etc., and away we went; sorry to have missed Christmas at home, but now determined to make up for it.

We were ferried ashore at Inveraray and began the long journey by coach to Glasgow. This time we went down the 'Rest and be Thankful' hill so at least we didn't have to get out and walk it. From Glasgow it was then homeward bound.

I had two hours to wait for my train and was undecided as to how to pass the time. I must have even 'looked' undecided because a lady, having seen my little silver Merchant Navy badge, stopped and kindly took me to a small canteen affair called Jock's Box. They were issuing free tea and sandwiches to service men, and each one was also given three cigarettes. This welcome interlude passed the time on nicely until my train was due. I was beginning to realise that there were kindly people in the world after all. I was also rather pleased at the attention I was given by these well-meaning Glasgow ladies. I think that in Glasgow, with its great shipbuilding traditions and seafaring history, the people were well aware of the contribution the merchant service was making, and it was gratifying to be on the receiving end of their gratitude.

At last my train arrived and I began my journey home. I arrived in Barrow at almost midnight, tired out but glad to be back. I had to walk home from the station, but was pleasantly surprised to find Mam and Jim still awake, and I detected a lot better atmosphere than on my previous leave.

I'd brought quite a few things home which were in short supply, but I think the one that Mam appreciated most was the two pounds of tea that I'd 'acquired'.

We sat up talking until almost daylight, catching up on everything that had happened to us all, and drinking tea with condensed milk, which made it feel like being back on board where all we had was 'conyony' as it was nicknamed.

Mam was now working for a Mrs Pank, doing cleaning and quite a bit of baby-sitting with her young children. Mr Pank was manager of the submarine yard at Vickers, and Mam seemed to get on well with them. They treated her more as a friend and confidant than simply an employee, and so they should have; she was a wise and resourceful person and I think they recognised these qualities.

Soon Jim would be off to the Royal Navy and I was glad that Mam had started to lead her life again after her upheavals. A lesser person would probably have yielded to self-pity.

All too soon my leave ended and it was time to go back to my ship. I'd thoroughly enjoyed my ten days and was going back in a much happier frame of mind than the last time I'd left Barrow. When I would return was anyone's guess; I could only hope it would not be too long.

The journey to Glasgow via Carnforth was uneventful, apart from a two hour wait for the bus to Inveraray, and I arrived back on board fourteen hours after leaving Barrow; tired, hungry and wondering where we were destined for next. Only time would tell.

12

The Events Leading up to 'Operation Ironclad'

If I had any doubts about having arrived back on board they were quickly and noisily dispelled at six o'clock next morning by the bo's'n's mate in charge of our watch. His chosen, and might I say very effective, method of 'Wakey! Wakey!' was to rattle a tin mug along the steel bars of our bunks while at the same time roaring at the top of his voice. Normally I quite liked the chap, but at six o'clock in the morning I could cheerfully have strangled him – though I'd have had to join the queue as everybody else felt the same.

After a quick mug of tea and a hastily sucked cigarette we were sent to anchor stations. We were off to Gourock at The Tail of The Bank to embark troops, and also to take on stores, etc. I don't know whether it was imagined or not, but there seemed to be an atmosphere that something different was afoot.

We reached our anchorage at last, which seemed to be much nearer the shore than the last time. It was bitterly cold and the weather took a turn for the worse. It blew a gale for over a week and all shipboard activity of an outside nature came to an end. There was no shore leave at all and we knew then that something important was definitely being planned.

At last the weather improved, wind-wise, but still didn't get any warmer. There were still flurries of sleet and snow, and the decks were like skating rinks. All our watches of four hours on and eight hours off were suspended, and except for eight men who were put on anchor watch the rest of us were to work from

d

daylight to dusk loading supplies from barges that were brought out to us. At the same time most of our lifeboats were taken away and in their places a newer type of landing craft were hoisted aboard. Any questions as to what this was all for were met by a silence from our officers that only meant one thing, they didn't know either.

The next thing was that a gang of tradesmen came aboard and started to build two large cradle structures, one each side of number one hold. It was obvious they were to hold some type of boat. The tradesmen worked at it for almost two weeks, and then one day just after they'd finished, two 'new' types of landing boats came alongside. They were flat-bottomed and the whole front end (bow) could be lowered to form a ramp. These were manned by Royal Navy lads.

The problem was how to get them aboard. Our ship had a large lifting derrick positioned on the foremast which was known as a Jumbo Derrick. This worked in conjunction with our winches, and when rigged it was capable of lifting fifty tons. When it was not in use it was fastened to the front of the mast by huge clamps, and my job was to help in getting it rigged ready to lift the two landing craft aboard. This we managed with a lot of sweat and cursing, and before long the two boats were safely on board and lashed down ready for our next destination – wherever that was.

The next day we raised anchor and steamed off through the lochs and braes of Bonnie Scotland. I can tell you that in that cold, miserable February and March 'bonnie' was the last description we'd have used for Scotland.

We anchored in Loch Fyne again, and that started the most intense and feverish few weeks we'd ever had. I felt sorry for the five hundred commandos we had on board, as they were subjected to the most gruelling training imaginable. Roused out of their sleep at about four o'clock in the morning and made to run to their landing craft, then put ashore in dark, inhospitable terrain to undergo various endurance tests. I thought, If they survive all this then the 'real thing' will be a walk-over. I needn't have worried because they seemed as hard as nails, and as they gradually became familiar with the whole operation they actually seemed to be enjoying themselves.

Another thing that impressed us all was the adaptability of the Royal Navy lads who manned the landing craft. When they'd arrived on board a few weeks earlier they'd seemed green and quite inexperienced, but now they were handling their craft like veterans, and had developed a great rapport with us merchant crewmen who raised and lowered their boats, also with the commandos themselves, who now always tried to make a beeline for their favourite boat.

Once again something my dad had said years before, struck me: "How could anyone allow men like these to rot in the misery of poverty and unemployment, when given the chance they could rise to any heights asked of them?" Once more I felt glad, and *yes* proud, to be working class. When I look back on that time in my life I remember all those lads and men. Their bravery, their laughter and their hopes, and I curse the glib politicians who let them down so badly when it was all over. All that talk about a country fit for heroes was just so much hot air from pygmies of men who weren't fit to lick these lads' boots.

The reader must forgive me these rantings. My excuse being that today as I write it is Remembrance Sunday, and at the moment I'm watching the brave, proud old men who once had wings on their heels, trudging past the Cenotaph with their heads held high on this their once-yearly recognition day – only to be conveniently forgotten again afterwards until next year

Now that I've got that off my chest I'll carry on with my memories.

March 1942 arrived, and someone on high must have been satisfied that ship and men were now ready for whatever was being planned. We were to have an official visit by some top brass, and typically we deck crew were set to painting, titivating and deck scrubbing until the day arrived. It turned out to be Lord Louis Mountbatten, dressed up like an admiral, with an entourage of top brass. They made a fleeting inspection of the men and ship, then departed to buck someone else's morale up. I didn't see any signs of that happening on the *Winchester Castle*, but I imagine these people have to justify their privileged positions somehow.

Some days later we had a visit from King George VI, and I and a Newfoundland seaman were chosen to go ashore in Loch Fyne to a place called Strachur, to be presented to him and to represent the ship's merchant seamen. This didn't take long, we simply lined up and he walked slowly past with his party. He stopped and spoke to one or two of the naval personnel, but then carried on past the rest of us. I was astonished to see how frail he looked, also that he was much smaller than I'd imagined. That then was my brush with royalty.

The next day we upped anchor and sailed to the Tail of The Bank and anchored off Gourock once more. Our commando passengers were disembarked and once more it was bedlam loading stores from lighters (barges) that were towed out to us. One of the senior stewards passed a remark that we had enough food on board to feed thousands. How true his words would become apparent the next day when a large tender called the *Palladin* came alongside carrying the first of the troops. They were lads from the East Lancashire Regiment and the *Palladin* made numerous trips between Gourock pier and the ship until the full regiment were on board. Then came all their equipment, and as we could only load in daylight hours it was a long drawn out process.

Lastly came our commandos, the Fifth, as we'd come to know them, and of course there were a lot of familiar faces from all the training exercises we'd taken them on in the lochs. It was now obvious that something was being planned in a big way.

We were soon joined at the anchorage by a lot more ships, and it was quickly noted by the more experienced seamen that all these new ships were of the fifteen to twenty-knot class, so we were obviously going to be a fast convoy. The puzzle, of course, was our destination.

Finally we weighed anchor and steamed down the Irish Sea, more or less in a long, straight line. We passed the Isle of Man on our starboard side in daylight, and I knew that over in the haze on our port side lay Walney Island, and beyond that my home town of Barrow. Although we couldn't see them, I couldn't help wondering when I would be back there again.

Soon afterwards another eight or nine ships joined us; I think they'd come out of the Mersey River, from either Liverpool or Birkenhead. These were followed by a cruiser and six destroyer escorts. Finally, as we proceeded down past the Bristol Channel two royal fleet auxiliary tankers completed the convoy; these were for the naval ships of course, to make sure they had enough fuel supplies for whatever eventualities we encountered.

The deck crew had reverted to watch-keeping which meant four hours on watch and eight hours off. My particular duties were as a lookout, and for the first few days we used the crow's nest on the foremast. Access to this was up a ladder of steel rungs welded to the fore part of the mast, and then through a trap door in the bottom of the crow's nest itself. As we ploughed on almost due west through the heavy Atlantic swells, this climb was pretty hazardous, because on reaching the trap door you had to bang on it for the lookout already there to open it up. You then had to squeeze awkwardly past one another as one went up the ladder and the other went down.

We were the commodore ship of the convoy. In other words the naval officers on board were in charge of the whole convoy. What rank these top brass were I don't know, but I guess the 'big shot' was a rear admiral. I seem to remember his name was Crumm, but I may be wrong. You see he wasn't exactly a gregarious chap, at least not with us deck crowd.

So the days passed, and we were zig-zagging constantly. By this time we must have been halfway across the Atlantic, but at long last we seemed to be turning south and rumour had it that we had taken this tortuous route to avoid running into an armed raider that had already sunk a lot of our shipping.

It must be remembered that at that time communications were relatively primitive, and in any case we had to maintain radio silence. There was no radar, and navigation was done by the sun whenever it showed, or by the stars on clear nights. Any information which had to be passed between our commodore ship and the escorts or other ships in the convoy was done by flag signals hoisted up the halyards to the top of the main mast. Each set of flags had its own coded meaning, and each ship had its code book to interpret them. All in all this proved very effective. We also had Aldis lamps to flash signals in morse code, but these were only used as a last resort, due to the fact that the slightest glimpse of light by a Jerry periscope would give our position away.

We were now getting confirmation of our southerly course, because the weather can't lie and it was getting warmer by the day.

About this time it was decided that all our lookouts would now be from the 'barrel'. This was called the barrel because that's exactly what it was, a steel barrel at the very top of the fore mast. It was thirty feet higher than the crow's nest and consequently gave a much wider view of the surrounding ocean. However, it was much harder to get to. We had to climb up the rigging that supports the mast, and then up a loose wire ladder to the barrel. The trick was to climb five or six rungs higher than the barrel to enable the lad who'd been on lookout in there for the previous two hours to climb out so that the new lookout could drop in. It was enough of an ordeal in daylight, but at night, feeling for hand and footholds in the dark, it was something of a scary gamble. A welcome bonus in all this was that after a two hour lookout in the barrel we were allowed a fifteen minute break for a smoke or hurried drink, before having to report to the bridge for further lookout duties and complete our four-hour watch.

In retrospect I can see the vital need for as many pairs of eyes as it was possible to use. We were in very hazardous waters and our officers and captain had the great responsibility of doing everything in their power to see the convoy safely to its destination. However, at the time we cursed this barrel duty roundly.

When I look back I've often wondered what these naval types thought of us, muffled up in all sorts of outlandish clothing. Whenever we reported for our spell of duty on the bridge there were always two of our own officers on watch, and most often our captain as well. In addition there'd be a very senior naval officer, plus his lackey and several naval rating signalmen all properly uniformed, of course. One of our shipmates who alternated watches with me, had a magnificent royal blue top coat almost down to his ankles; some relative of his had been a commissionaire at a cinema. It still had the huge shoulder epaulettes on it and 'Gaumont Cinemas' in gold braid on the lapels. The first time he went on watch dressed in it the rear admiral almost had an apoplectic fit. He must have thought he was hallucinating. The quartermaster who was at the wheel at the time, told me that he didn't stop spluttering for an hour. What made it worse was that every time he looked out of the wheel-house door he could see this vision in royal blue out there at his lookout station. The seaman himself had no idea that anyone could take exception to what after all was a good, warm coat, even if it was somewhat garish.

Sometime later we were told by the captain's 'tiger' (valet – most large passenger ships pre-war looked after their captains very well, and a valet was one of their perks) that he'd overheard the rear admiral asking if the 'merchant crew' could show a little more deference in their dress, etc., and our captain had given him short shrift. The gist of this being that when all was said and done we were vital civilians and as such had to provide our own clothing for whatever climate we found ourselves in at our own expense, while the bulk of our wages were remitted to our dependents; wives, mothers, etc. He also told the rear admiral – and I admired him greatly for this – that the lad in the blue coat was a fine seaman, and he wouldn't dream of hurting his feelings over something so trivial. They say that from then on the previous cordiality they'd enjoyed was a bit strained. Later the captain was heard to remark, that in any event they should have showed the merchant lad more respect because he had more gold braid on his 'commissionaire's' coat than they had on theirs.

So the voyage went on. The weather was wonderful and before long we rounded the Cape of Good Hope, but avoided Cape Town. Once more speculation was rife as to what our final port of call would be. At this stage the ship was being lifted like a cork by huge waves although the weather was perfect. The ship's movement was quite upsetting as there seemed to be no visible signs of what was causing it. One of our old hands who'd spent a lifetime at sea hazarded a guess, which later proved correct, that as we were between the South African coast and Antarctica these huge waves were the result of violent storms further south.

We were all relieved when the convoy finally turned north and we left these huge rollers far behind. I noticed then, and I saw it many times later, that sometimes the sea can take on a menacing appearance. It has something to do with weather far away, and great depths which combine to create a sense of foreboding. I for one was glad to see the coastline of Africa, it gave back a sense of reality – I think we're always apprehensive when faced with something we can't understand.

So once again we docked in Durban, although this time we were not allowed ashore. Naturally we were disappointed, but had to make the best of it.

After taking on supplies of food and fuel oil we set sail once more and passed the Bluff where The Lady In White sang to us again her repertoire of patriotic songs. As usual she brought a lump to my throat, and I'm sure in her own way she did a lot for morale.

The convoy was now being led by an old battleship, the *Ramillies*, but 'we' were still the commodore ship leading all the merchantmen. Our troops, the East Lancashire Regiment, and the Fifth Commando lads were on deck every day and seemed to be rehearsing for some activity that was still not obvious. This was one of my pet grumbles with those in authority; it was never thought necessary to explain anything to the very people who were involved. We were treated as though we were incapable of coherent thought.

There was no attempt at zig-zagging by the convoy now as we sailed north, and at dusk on the third or 4th of May 1942 my ship, the *Winchester Castle*, and a lean looking light cruiser broke away from the rest of the ships and headed at a top speed of over twenty knots into the Mozambique Channel; this runs between the African mainland and the Island of Madagascar. Soon all was made clear. At around midnight on the 5th of May we altered course to the east and we, the deck crew, were sent to our stations ready to offload the two large landing craft when the order was given. Our speed was cut and the cruiser stayed out in the open sea, while we slowly edged into what turned out to be Courier Bay, an inlet on the northern coast on Madagascar.

Here we quickly dropped anchor and proceeded to put the two landing craft over the side. Once they were in the water our commando lads swarmed over the ship's side down into them and away they went. It wasn't until later that we found out they were to march overland and spike some guns that were a threat to what was to be our main landing.

When the landing craft returned after putting the commandos ashore we hoisted the craft aboard again, raised the anchor and sailed around the north of the island to our next destination, Diego Suarez, where the main landing by our East Lancashire Regiment was to take place.

For the next week we worked feverishly unloading supplies etc., to enable the soldiers to consolidate a bridgehead. It was only then that we learned that the commandos had not managed to arrive in time to spike the guns. It appeared that the difficulty of the terrain they'd been expected to traverse had been wildly underestimated by our intelligence sources, and the lads were days late. Fortunately the the East Lancs had silenced the guns themselves.

By this time, approximately 12th of May, our troops had secured an airfield so that our planes could land from East Africa to give air cover to the further advances which would lead to our complete control of the whole island. At that time the French troops who garrisoned Madagascar were supporters of Vichy France. They fought doggedly, but were overcome after fierce fighting and casualties were high.

The following day was my nineteenth birthday, and I remember thinking, 'Here we go again. Why do I always spend my birthdays in some outlandish spot where I'm unable to celebrate?'

However, there was not much time to worry as news was coming in, from where I don't know, that some form of Japanese fleet was heading towards us. And now it became obvious why we'd taken the island in the nick of time. If the Japs had beaten us to it the consequences would have been catastrophic. Their navy would have been able to dominate the Indian Ocean and thus prevent any supplies reaching our North African or Far Eastern campaigns. Had they managed to land a decent-sized force on Madagascar with its mountainous, dense jungle conditions I don't think we could have defeated them for years.

It then emerged that all the bombs and ammunition for our Royal Air Force friends were down in our number two cargo hold, so we were all set to unloading this and getting it ashore as fast as possible. Of course, we were limited by the speed of our winches, and it turned out to be a long, wearying few days with no rest at all. We worked day and night until finally the last bombs were ashore and we were allowed to relax a little for a few days. I was unlucky once again because I was a winch driver and had to stand by to take our landing craft on board whenever they came back alongside with injured men, or to take more supplies ashore. Between trips I dozed at the winch controls.

After a while things seemed to be quietening down ashore, apart from some sporadic small arms fire. I suppose the East Lancs were pressing inland and southwards to link up with other troops who'd been landed further down the coast.

However, the lull was short lived, for during the night of the 29th of May two Japanese midget submarines crept into Diego Suarez Bay and torpedoed the battleship *Ramillies*. She was anchored about a thousand yards from us and the explosions were earsplitting. There was frenzied activity all around. A destroyer, HMS *Anthony*, which had taken part in the initial landings with us, began circling around dropping depth charges, but whether they ever found the midget submarines we never heard. The battleship was listing badly but didn't seem to be in any danger of sinking. I think there were casualties aboard her, but the extent of them remained a mystery.

About an hour after the *Ramillies* was struck, another midget submarine torpedoed and sank the tanker *British Loyalty*. All this inside Diego Suarez Bay which should have been enemy proof. The following week the *Ramillies* set off with an escort, probably to Durban. I never saw her again but I think that after repairs she saw the end of the war.

These events shook the authorities into belated action, and now that Madagascar was secure in allied hands we weighed anchor and made for Durban at rib-rattling full speed. As I said earlier in this chapter, this was the first successful capture of an enemy stronghold, and I'm not alone when I say that it secured our supply routes to North Africa and to the Far East now that the Mediterranean was closed.

So ended 'Operation Ironclad'.

Subsequently our ship, the *Winchester Castle*, and her crew were awarded 'Battle Honours', which was the equivalent of being 'mentioned in dispatches' to service personnel. The most bizarre outcome of this was that our bo's'n, an Ulster man, was awarded the George Cross, which is the highest award available to a civilian, when from beginning to end of the action he'd been confined to his bunk with tropical influenza. I've often wondered if he ever tells the true story. Still, he had done enough beforehand to merit it, so we all said good luck to him.

Once again we docked in Durban, South Africa, but this trip we were allowed shore leave, and apart from our daily work deck scrubbing, painting, etc., we were free from five o'clock each evening and had a thoroughly enjoyable ten days in what was then a lovely city.

The only blot on the landscape for me was once again seeing how much the opulent life-style enjoyed by the white population was in contrast to the abject poverty lived in by the true inhabitants. The foundations of apartheid in all its selfish rottenness were evident even then. The signs were everywhere (literally). 'Whites Only' notices were posted in toilets, bars, buses, etc. It seemed a sick irony that in their own land the black people were reduced to living in isolated ghettos. And the thing I found most repulsive was the fact that the white population seemed to accept all this as if it was the natural order of life. What a travesty of justice it all was.

At last our brief, partial holiday came to an end. The ship was stocked up again with food and fuel, and loaded to the gunnels with troops and their equipment. Of course, the inevitable guessing game began once more. It was easier this time, however, as it must either be up the Red Sea to Egypt, or across the Indian Ocean to Bombay.

As we sailed out of Durban we told the army lads to keep their eyes on the Bluff, the finger of land which had once been an old whaling station, and there, sure enough, was the Lady in White singing her heart out to boost our morale as usual, and bringing a lump to many a throat. She never let us down.

13

Once More to Destinations Unknown

So we left Durban and the Lady in White, and once more headed out into the Indian Ocean, our destination still a mystery to a certain degree, but as mentioned already, at that point in the war it was almost certainly through the Red Sea to Egypt, or to Bombay, to reinforce either the Middle East or the Far East.

We'd formed a loose convoy with four other ships, and we were the commodore ship again. As escort we had a light cruiser, leading, and two destroyers, one on either side of us, and as we were moving at about eighteen knots we felt comparatively secure.

On our port side was one of the nicest-looking ships I'd ever seen. She was a Polish vessel, the *Sobieski*. I'll bet that before the war when she was painted in her company colours she'd been a grand sight. Even now in drab grey she was striking. On our starboard side was a twelve-thousand ton heavy lifting ship. She had huge derricks (Jumbos) that could lift over 150 tons. Her name was the *Clan McGregor*. What her hold cargo was I don't know, but on deck lashed down with chains and wires were two railway locomotives. Where they were bound we couldn't guess – until our destination became clearer.

During the early part of the voyage the troops, who were our passengers, would often buttonhole any member of the deck crew who happened to be working on deck to see if we knew the final port of call. Of course we couldn't enlighten them though we tried, at least *I* did, to say anything that might make them less apprehensive. It wasn't always successful, but we tried.

When I look back to that time, July 1942, I think it was then that I began to realise the enormity of the war. We had endless discussions off watch as to how it was shaping, either in the allies favour or not.

The previous year had seen Hitler launch Operation Barbaros' (Red Beard), and now the German Army was simply racing into the Soviet Union, and it seemed they were invincible. The Japanese were dominating the whole of the Pacific theatre. They'd taken Malaya and Singapore along with thousands of allied prisoners. These poor lads were destined to face years of barbarism and suffering at the hands of an inhuman and cruel captor who thought nothing of the Geneva Convention. Though we obviously didn't know this at the time.

The allies had already lost two prized capital ships; the battleship *Prince of Wales* and the battle cruiser *Repulse* to Japanese bombing and torpedo attacks. Both of these vessels were destroyed with an appalling loss of lives. It also stunned the top brass at the admiralty and elsewhere, who couldn't conceive of any nation challenging the Rule Britannia naval superiority attitude that prevailed at that time. Some of those in charge were still fighting the previous war's battles, and thought it was just a matter of sending a gunboat to quell the restless natives. As *this* war progressed, however, they were in for shock after shock as all the old theories were being demolished – almost daily.

I think that if these 'Colonel Blimps' and 'Jutland Johnnies' had been pensioned off, and younger ideas adopted from the beginning, the war would have ended a lot sooner.

An example was Josip Broz Tito, who by using the guerrilla tactics of 'strike and run' was holding three German divisions at bay in Yugoslavia. The Germans badly needed these divisions elsewhere, but daren't move them or they'd have lost the Balkans completely.

However, as far as these Blimps were concerned guerrilla tactics weren't taught at the Sandhurst Military Academy so that was that. Unfortunately it wasn't until the relatively young Orde Wingate came along with similar ideas to Tito that guerrilla warfare was eventually faced up to and accepted.

Our destination was now apparent, and although we were still zig-zagging during daylight hours, our course was predominantly eastwards, so unless we were diverted to Ceylon it looked like Bombay once more. It was obvious that most of our troops were destined for the Fourteenth Army – or the Forgotten Army as they came to be known later. Fighting disease, Malaria and the Japanese in the jungles of Burma was not a very enviable prospect. We never commented on any of this to them, of course. They had enough to contend with, what with non commissioned-officers who were bullies, and commissioned officers who for the most part were only officers because they had the 'correct' social background and had been to decent – i.e. public – schools. I suppose that the law of averages would ensure that at least some of them would turn out OK, but in those early days the rest were rubbish.

I remember something that George Bernard Shaw had once said when some oaf insisted haughtily that public schools taught their intake to be 'leaders of men'. He replied, "Yes, and the elementary schools teach *their* pupils to be 'led' – mindlessly."

I think in this the Royal Navy had a better record. Their officer class at least had a decent grounding in things nautical, and to a larger degree were appointed on merit. At least, the ones I came into contact with seemed to have been.

So at long last we arrived in Bombay and tied up in the Alexander Docks. Then began the job of disembarking our troops and hundreds of tons of equipment. We had another four holds full of supplies for the vast army of men and women stationed all over India and Burma. It was a long-winded procedure, and when it was completed we would then have to start the same process in reverse; loading more cargo and personnel for our next port of call. Which inevitably started up the old guessing game about destination.

Looking back to those far off days we seemed to spend half our spare time mulling over what cargo we were carrying and what type of passengers we'd embarked, in order to glean a little inkling as to our next destination. Unfortunately we were nearly always wrong.

During our time in Bombay on that particular occasion my pal, Hendricks, and I decided to have a meal at one of the best hotels in the city. The best of all was the Taj Mahal Hotel, but it was way out of our price range, so we settled on one known simply as Greens. It was well worth the visit. The meal, though still expensive, was marvellous and worth every penny; if only to see how the Indian upper class lived.

Sitting at the next table to us was a Dutch family who had apparently escaped from Sumatra. The man was something in the consular service, and as I've said earlier my pal Hendricks was fluent in Dutch, so he was soon in animated conversation with them all. They quickly seemed to lose their initial nervousness and we all had a great night. I know Hendricks did as he was delighted to be able to show off his linguistic prowess. Little did we know then, that when we sailed we'd have this family aboard and that Hendricks would do all he could to make their voyage pleasurable.

At last the ship was fully laden once more. Hatches were battened down, lifting derricks stowed and everything that needed to be lashed down was. It only remained for our passengers to embark.

The first aboard were about one hundred WRNS, WAAFS and nurses, all in various stages of pregnancy. At that time, of course, they were treated with disdain; luckily times and attitudes have changed since then. They were followed by soldiers who'd been ill and were no longer fit for active service. Most of them had the pallor that comes from numerous attacks of malaria or other debilitating tropical ailments. Some were limbless, and I wondered what sort of life they were going home to face after giving their service to His Majesty. All of these were taken to parts of the ship that had been turned into temporary sick bays. The rest of the embarkees were civilians of various nationalities, and some, like our Dutch acquaintances, were families.

We were soon ready for sea once more, and this time I think everyone on board was hoping that it would be Blighty and home.

The night before we sailed, one of our quartermasters, whose only duty aboard was to steer the ship and keep the bridge and chartroom tidy, fell badly as he was coming back aboard and broke both his arm and collar bone. There were some uncharitable people, and some of a vindictive nature who suggested it was due to the fact that he was drunk. What . . ! A British merchant seaman in a foreign port getting drunk! I don't believe it. All that I will say is that when we carried him, moaning with pain, down to the sick bay his breath would have stripped paint.

The result of this was that as we were now a quartermaster short I was seconded to the job. I thought right from the start that it would be the most tedious duty on the ship, but I couldn't refuse. So on the following day I was at the wheel as we sailed from Bombay. My duties involved doing two hours at the wheel, followed by two hours as lookout outside on the wing of the bridge.

Our watch was from eight to twelve, which on merchant ships was traditionally the watch when the second officer, or 'mate' was in charge. He also acted, and was known as, 'the navigating officer' being responsible for plotting the ship's position at noon every day. Naturally the skipper and first mate also took their own sextant readings during daylight, or astral (star) readings at night – in those days satellites were the stuff of science fiction, and a ship's position was determined by these sextant observations plus the readings from the ship's 'log'; which was a device towed from the ship's stern and connected to a clock which recorded the ship's mileage. However, in bad weather, when sun and star readings were not possible, a system known as 'dead reckoning' was used. This involved calculating tidal currents and drift as well as mileage from the log, and in nine cases out of ten these navigators could position a ship to within a five-mile square of ocean under these conditions.

Just as I'd thought, after about three days in my new job as quartermaster I was bored to tears and looking for a chance of escape. Finally, at noon one day, when we were a few days out from Bombay, my chance came from a most unexpected source. The weather was wonderful, and on this particular day the officers were assembled to make the day's sextant reading, when the captain came into the wheel-house. He gave me a peculiar look and asked, "How's your head?" – he wasn't being suddenly solicitous about my health, he was just asking me in nautical parlance what course I was steering. He then asked me where my hat was. I told him quite honestly that I didn't possess one. At this he frowned then went out to join the chief and second officer on the bridge wing.

Some time later as I was relieved at the wheel by the next watch and about to make my way to our quarters, I found the chief officer waiting for me in the fo'c'sle. He told me that when I'd had my dinner I was to go along to what was called the

'Slops', which was a sort of shipboard stores where we bought cigarettes, chocolate, etc; the cost of which would be deducted from our wages at the end of the voyage. He said I was to get a navy style hat, with Union Castle headband, plus two pairs of blue trousers and two white shirts. This was, as the chief put it, "to make me look like a quartermaster." I then asked him who would pay for them, and he replied, "Don't worry, they'll be deducted from your pay when the ship reaches the UK and pays off."

I don't know where I got the nerve from when I look back, but as I was heartily sick of the job I plucked up the courage from somewhere and said, "No, sir, I don't want any new trousers and shirts, and I certainly don't want a naval type hat." And in a rush of bravado I added, "I also don't want to look like a quartermaster, because I didn't want the job in the first place. I'd sooner be back on my normal deck duties."

I thought at first from the expression on his face that he would have me up before the captain for my impudence. But after a moment he just grinned – I think that was the first time I'd seen him smile – then he said, "All right, young man, report to the bo's'n that you are back on normal duties. And tell him to find another candidate for the 'lousy job' you so detest."

I thanked him and scarpered as fast as I could. I couldn't wait to tell my mates of my lucky escape. Being a quartermaster definitely wasn't my cup of tea; there wasn't enough activity.

So the voyage continued, and at last we reached Durban again where we were in for a surprise that would effect every one of our passengers, who, like us, were under the impression that we were headed for the UK and home.

We docked at Point Docks and all our passengers were disembarked and transferred to other ships for the rest of their journey. Where we were bound still remained a mystery. But, with all the optimism of youth we took it all in our stride. We were in a lovely port, the weather was good, so as sailors the world over we made the most of today, and let tomorrow worry about itself. An old seaman once told me that the seagoing fraternity wish their lives away. If they're at sea they wish they were ashore, and when they're ashore, and broke, they wish they were at sea; and I think that just about sums up life at sea.

At last the ship was ready for sea and I'd never seen her so quiet. The only people on board were a party of Americans who kept themselves to themselves. They all wore civilian dress and had all their meals together at the captain's table in the main or first class dining-room. We never did find out who they were, but one snippet of gossip came from a waiter who served them at dinner one night. Apparently they were asking the skipper what his plans would be if it looked as if Britain would fall, and where would he take his ship. I believe he just smiled at them and wise, patriotic old bird that he was, told them the question was barmy as Britain would never fall, and apparently stopped that speculation dead in its tracks. At that time, eight months after Pearl Harbour had brought America into the war, it still wasn't clear how far America would go to support the European war while their main enemy was the Japanese. Only time would tell.

So finally we sailed from South Africa, still uncertain as to where we were going, but wherever it was we were sailing alone; no convoy this trip, and apart from the twenty Americans we were like a ghost ship compared to previous voyages. I remember that the weather was perfect, and it was a pleasure to be on normal duties instead of confined to the wheel-house as I had been.

At the end of two days it was fairly obvious that we were were heading for the Americas, either North or South. We were sailing directly into the sun and were still well to the south of the Atlantic, and also sailing at full speed. We'd been under the impression that the Germans had no U-boats as far south as this, but the following day we found out differently.

The next day I was on the twelve to four watch with my pal Hendricks. We were on the fo'c'sle splicing an eye back into a mooring rope which had snapped when we were leaving Durban. From two until four I was due to do a two hour stint on lookout up in the crow's-nest, but at about one o'clock the lad who was already up in the crow's-nest called out that he'd seen an object two points on the starboard bow, but was unable to make out what it was. There was a heavy swell running, but otherwise visibility was perfect. The next moment the chief officer, using a loudhailer or megaphone, shouted down, "Workman . . ! Get up into the top barrel as fast as you can and see if you can make out what it is."

I needed no second telling and in less than a minute I was up in the barrel, which was a lot higher vantage point than the main crow's-nest. From there I could see, rolling in the swell, what appeared to be an empty lifeboat about a mile away. As quickly as I could I climbed down to the deck again, dashed up to the bridge and reported what I'd seen to the chief. By this time he'd been joined by the captain, and they went into a huddle out on the wing of the bridge. The captain had a very grave decision to make; this could be a decoy, and some U-boat skipper might at that moment be lining his periscope up for a significant 'kill', as they called it. On the other hand, if there was life aboard the lifeboat he had a seaman's moral duty to attempt a rescue.

He stood there like a statue for what seemed ages, but at last he made up his mind. "Young man," he said to me, "get down to the well deck and inform the bo's'n that I want a grab net hung over the side, and you younger sailors ready to go down it if there proves to be anyone in the lifeboat. I think that with his experienced eye, and of course powerful binoculars, he'd seen some movement and was ready to gamble that he could rescue them and be off before anything could happen.

Our course was altered and our speed gradually cut until we slowly brought the grab-net hanging over the side as close to the lifeboat as we could. We could now see that there were men lying in the bottom of it and as it bumped alongside, myself and another lad scrambled gingerly down the grab-net to try to secure mooring lines to each end of the boat. It was a precarious job because the heavy swell was heaving the lifeboat up about fifteen feet and then dropping it down again.

We finally got our lines attached and could then set about getting the poor devils lying in the bottom on board. Nearly all of them were in a kind of coma, so ropes with running nooses were passed down to us. Then, with pulling from above, and the two of us giving a lift from behind we managed to get them all aboard one by one. The frenzied activity seemed to have roused most of them quite a bit, and they were able to help themselves up the net, to some extent at least. The last two, however, were totally unconscious and we had to virtually carry them up to safety. With them all aboard, the lifeboat was cut adrift and the DEMS gunners – the Royal Navy lads who manned our guns – got in a bit of useful target practice sinking it.

It had taken about ten minutes for the whole rescue to be completed, but I swear the old captain had aged ten years while his ship was stationary and a sitting target. Our bo's'n, who was now a proud George Medalist, paid a lovely complement to him. He said, "That if he never did another kindly deed in his life, he's done his share by having the courage to save these sailors lives."

It turned out that the survivors, all Americans, had been part of the crew of an American Freighter named the SS *Honoluluan*. They'd been en route from Cape Town to Baltimore when at dawn ten days earlier they'd been torpedoed and left to drift in a lifeboat by a ruthless member of the 'master race'. The reader will gather again that I detest submarine warfare. If we hadn't spotted that boat by the strangest of chances they would almost certainly have died, because in all that vast expanse of the South Atlantic I'll bet we were the only passing ship. These nine lads were all that was left of a crew of thirty-five; the rest having gone to a watery grave.

By this time we were bucketing along again at about twenty knots and still wondering where to. Reports from the sick bay were promising, as most of the survivors were responding to medical treatment, though the two who'd been unconscious were still very poorly. One of them had been bitten very badly by a shark and had lost a lot of blood. There was no shortage of volunteers to be donors and he seemed to be holding his own. In those days donors lay on another bed alongside the recipient and the blood was passed via a tube straight from one to the other. Primitive perhaps, but in this case proving effective.

It appeared that at the moment of impact by the torpedo, this man had been out on deck and was thrown overboard. After the ship had sunk and while only semi-conscious he'd managed to find a wooden hatch board, and had clung onto it through that day and the next night. When the rest of the survivors, in the one lifeboat they'd managed to launch, found him he was actually being attacked by a shark, because his legs were dangling in the sea. They managed to beat off the shark with boat hooks and an oar and get him into the boat. These lads at that time were quite fit of course, but when we found them ten days later they were in a sorry state; ravenously hungry and quite dehydrated . . . man's inhumanity to man.

Finally we reached the Ambrose Light and knew at last that we were bound for New York. To say that we were excited is an understatement. After growing up watching films about Broadway and the skyscrapers, and listening on the radio to the boxing contests from Madison Square Gardens, this was like a dream come true.

We sailed past the Statue of Liberty and into the Hudson River with the huge Department of Immigration Airship hovering just above us. As we nosed slowly up river about eight of the smallest tugs I'd ever seen came bustling around us. They didn't take a line aboard as is usual practice, but simply nudged us with their heavily fendered bows into pier ninety, which pre-war had been used only by the Cunard Company's big ocean liners.

As we came slowly alongside to tie up, it became obvious that some event was about to take place on the quayside. A gangway was lifted into position and secured, then about ten men in white uniforms came aboard first and were escorted below by one of our officers. They emerged with our American survivors; two on stretchers and the rest following. On the quayside the activity was hectic. Apparently any American merchant seaman who was mined or torpedoed received a cheque from the US Government for five thousand dollars.

The reception they were given was an eye-opener to us. Before our eyes they were being photographed and having their stories taken down by about thirty news reporters. It was unbelievable, they were being treated like royalty. Another curious feature was that the lad who'd been bitten by a shark was being interviewed separately. We learned later that these interviewers were representatives of a man called Ripley who ran a syndicated news feature which appeared in most American newspapers at that time. This feature was under the heading, 'Believe It Or Not', and apparently Ripley had once claimed in it that no one had ever been bitten by a shark and survived, and that he had witnesses to prove it. This lad had obviously disproved that, and Ripley presented him with another five thousand dollars for proving him wrong. What a country.

After our mooring was completed, all of us who'd taken part in rescuing them, twelve in all, were lined up at the top of the gangway and given a lovely vote of thanks by a man who we assumed was from the US Government. We were also given an envelope each, containing twenty-five dollars and an invitation to visit the USO any time we were ashore in New York – this was the United Services Organisation who looked after the needs of all service men, providing free tickets to most events occurring in

New York. Believe me we were as proud as punch. This was a recognition, or appreciation, that we would never have received in the UK and we all intended to enjoy it to the full. We couldn't wait to get ashore.

To mention the generosity of the Americans to their merchant seamen brings into sharp contrast the treatment meted out to the British seamen by the authorities in the UK at that time. If a British seaman was mined or torpedoed his pay was stopped at that moment, and if he was fortunate enough to be rescued, and many thousands were not, he was given a week's survivor's leave and the grand sum of . . . wait for it . . . thirteen pounds and fifteen shillings to replace all his lost clothing. As was made clear to me more than once: we were, after all, civilians. The clothing we were expected to provide for ourselves had to cover every kind of climatic eventuality, from arctic conditions to temperate or tropical. This was for the simple reason that we 'civilians' never knew where we would get sent to from one ship to the next. What a miserly attitude in comparison with America.

After all the excitement of that day, with our welcoming committee etc., we woke up next morning to find we were leaving pier ninety and moving to a naval dockyard for extensive additions to the ship's fire power. It looked as if the *Winchester Castle* was going to be turned into a semi-armed cruiser, and would be involved in a lot more hazardous operations in the future.

Eventually we were moored in Brooklyn Navy Yard, and had hardly put a gangway ashore when hundreds of shipyard workers literally swarmed aboard with typical American efficiency, and gangs were landing skips of equipment on deck for what was obviously going to be a huge job.

The dockyard people were going to fit two large guns to the fo'c'sle head (the front end of the ship) as well as gun nests all along the upper decks for anti-aircraft guns. These were to be fitted with Swedish Oerlikon guns, which had a rapid fire and seemed to be very efficient. We already had Bofors guns aft, and our main six-inch naval gun on the stern of the ship. I was a member of the the six-inch gun grew, which was led by a Royal Navy gunlayer who was a real stickler for efficiency. By the time all this new arsenal was installed we'd certainly be able to make a lot of noise, and hopefully able to defend our ship against enemy warships and planes if necessary.

In the meantime, however, while all of this activity was going on we were to live ashore in a hotel until the heavy work was finished. This was because our accommodation was all in the forward part of the ship right where the decks had to be strengthened to support the new heavy guns.

This trip was turning out to be better than anything we could have hoped for; an impromptu holiday in a New York hotel and quite a few dollars to spend. We also had our ticket to the USO which we intended to use to the full and see as much of the city as possible.

On arrival in New York we had all received quite a lot of letters from home, which had been chasing us around the world, fortunately most of them contained good news. I remember thinking that if the hotel had a writing room I'd be able to sit in comfort to answer them, instead of perched on my bunk in our cramped and ill-lit cabin with inquisitive shipmates looking over my shoulder.

We were eventually taken to the Hotel Albert on Eighth Street, Manhattan Island. We all had separate rooms, which unaccustomed as we were to privacy of any sort was a real treat in itself. And as this was obviously the first time I'd ever stayed in a hotel anyway, I was determined to enjoy every moment, observing how the better off took this sort of thing for granted.

I think, looking back, that at that moment I began to appreciate what being a sailor really meant. The long hours of drudgery, painting, scraping rust and red-leading; the cold, miserable watches either up in the crow's-nest or out on the wing of a windswept bridge, all seemed worth while when the prize at the end was shore time in exotic ports and breathtaking places like New York. I don't think I'd ever been so excited as I was that day. I and all my mates were determined to see everything that was worth seeing.

We were taken by coach from Brooklyn Navy Yard to our hotel on Eighth Street, and as we drove along every eye was at the windows to see all we could. When we arrived at the Albert Hotel it seemed as though the entire staff was there to greet us. We were all taken individually to our rooms which to me seemed palatial. We were told to settle in and lunch would be served in the hotel dining-room in thirty minutes. This was treatment we'd never expected, and at times I thought it was all a dream.

The lunch was absolutely wonderful. First we had a soup that I'd never heard of, but which tasted delicious. This was followed by a huge steak with mushrooms and French fried potatoes which in our ignorance we called chips. For dessert we had a choice of ice creams that again were new to us, or cherry pie. I chose the pie and was astonished at the size of the portions. It was as thick as a the sole of a surgical boot, and was accompanied by a jug of thick cream. What a meal! And what an introduction to American cuisine.

We all trooped out of the dining-room and were asked to assemble in the hotel lounge. As I felt like a poisoned pup by this time I was only too glad to relax in a comfortable chair to hear what our guide had to say. He first gave us a sensible pep-talk on the many pitfalls we could perhaps meet, and how to avoid them. Ladies of the night, and con-men figured large amongst his warnings, but he added that we, as merchant seamen, were held in such high esteem that he didn't think we would come to any harm.

He finally gave us a hotel brochure which had a really useful, easy to follow map on the back with our hotel's location clearly marked. I still have mine, though how I've managed to keep it all this time I don't know. Then off we went on a voyage of discovery.

My memories of that first day are of complete awe. The whole city seemed to be a bustle of energy, and Hendricks and I were like two kids let loose in a chocolate factory. Everything seemed so much larger than life, that compared to the shortages and drabness of life at home it was a revelation.

First we walked to Broadway, known in those days as 'The Great White Way', and as dusk descended and thousands of neon signs lit up it was obvious why it was so called. The sidewalks were crowded with people out for their evening entertainment, and we were content just to be a part of it all. We stopped at the huge bar and restaurant of Jack Dempsey – the ex-heavyweight champion of the world – and as visiting seamen we were welcomed like long lost relations. Unfortunately Jack Dempsey was away on business, so we never saw him. However, we were given souvenir postcards with his photo on them to fill in and send home to let our people know we were well. Sadly these cards were confiscated later by our ship's security conscious officers, who thought that if they fell into enemy hands they would give away the ship's location and our purpose for being in New York. With the large number of German sympathisers there were in the States, I would imagine that Jerry already knew more about our visit than we did anyway. At least Lord Haw Haw always seemed to be well informed, because whenever he broadcast from Germany, he appeared to know our convoy movements as well as we did.

That was our first day in New York, and we made our way back to the hotel tired out and floating on cloud nine, but working out plans for the next day.

The following morning's breakfast, was again an eye-opener as far as both quality and quantity were concerned, with orange juice, ham and eggs, delicious potato cakes and coffee that tasted like nothing I'd ever tasted before. I thought if coffee tastes like this I don't think I'll drink tea again. So once again full of good food, we set off first of all to find the USO to take up the invitation we'd been given. We eventually found it on Forty-Second Street, and after explaining who we were, and how we'd got our invite in the first place, we were welcomed with kindness and genuine warmth by the staff; who were incidentally all volunteers. We were given a quantity of tokens for free travel on the underground railway, and a bunch of tickets that would give us access to various places of interest which we were dying to visit.

The one place that was uppermost in our minds was the Empire State Building. I'd heard and read so much about it, as well as seen it in the original *King Kong* film when he'd climbed up it, that this was an absolute must for a visit. We took to the subway and though at first we found it puzzling we gradually gained confidence as to which trains to catch. In any case there was no shortage of advice as most New Yorkers were more than helpful, and soon we found ourselves standing at the entrance to the Empire State Building eagerly waiting for the lifts (elevators) to the top. The first lift took us to the forty-fifth floor (I think) where we had to change for the final ascent. This was the first time in my life that I'd ever been in a lift, and here I was using them in what was at that time the tallest building in the world. The Empire Sate was then only about ten years old, and was still seen as an

e

engineering marvel. Believe me, to us it was all that and more.

At last we came out onto the observation platform, which I think was about the ninety-something floor. The view was amazing, and sited around the platform were telescopes which operated with a nickel in the slot (five cents). These enabled you to see for about fifty miles in every direction. Fascinating as it was we had to tear ourselves away, because we had a lot more to see, and wanted to fit in as much as we could.

The descent in the lifts was another experience in itself. It felt as if the bottom had dropped out as we plummeted at what speed I don't know. And yet we experienced no feelings of apprehension. We knew instinctively that it was safe, or at least wishfully convinced ourselves that it was.

And so it was back down into the subway again. By this time we'd discovered that there were two different companies operating the underground and that they apparently served different areas. We never quite figured out which was which, but as they both accepted our tokens it didn't matter. Our next trip was to the Bronx Park Zoo, where one of the star attractions was a gorilla name Gargantua. It was massive. Almost seven feet tall, and as broad as it was long. The story on a plaque outside its cage explained that it had once been owned privately by some lady, but as it grew it became savage. It had attacked either its owner or an attendant, so had to be restrained and placed in captivity at the zoo. One of my daughters told me recently that she'd seen a film called Buddy, which was apparently a biography of the woman who'd raised this gorilla in the mistaken belief that she could domesticate it. Obviously she never succeeded.

The rest of the day spent at the zoo was great. It also gave us our introduction to another American institution, the humble hotdog, and we certainly did them justice. I must have eaten twenty during the course of that day.

Eventually it was back to the hotel via the subway, on which we were now becoming seasoned travellers. At the hotel we had to relate our experiences to our guide over dinner, and he told us that he'd lived in New York all his life, but had never been to the Bronx Park Zoo or the Empire State Building, and had never even heard of Gargantua.

And so the week passed. Every day we were off after breakfast to some of the places that were recommended to us; Washington

Square, Greenwhich Village, the Bohemian Quarter etc. We took the subway to Harlem, where incidentally we never heard an unwelcoming word and were treated marvellously; the little silver merchant navy badge seemed to be an 'open sesame' everywhere we went.

Our time passed all too quickly, and unfortunately the day arrived when we had to return to the ship. It appeared that nearly all the work had been done, so obviously we'd have to start the big clean-up and get her ready for sea again.

On the day of our departure from the hotel, the manager was at breakfast and wished us all well for the future, but he added a rider to his good wishes that puzzled us. He said he didn't think he'd seen the last of us. We wondered at the time if he knew more than he was letting on, and later that day we were to find out that he was right.

We arrived back at the shipyard to discover scenes of utter chaos. Our accommodation was a shambles because all the bunks had been removed in order to install the huge steel support beams needed to strengthen the deck above where the two heavy gun platforms had been located. Added to this was all the paraphernalia lying around associated with any major alteration of this kind. It was pretty obvious that we couldn't return to the ship while this situation continued, and it looked as if someone had slipped up in ordering us back.

While we were waiting for someone to issue sensible instructions we decided to have a look at what our cabin would be like once the shipyard workers had finished. It wasn't a very reassuring sight. We'd been cramped enough before, but after this we'd barely have access to our bunks, and certainly no room to move about in.

One of the Americans saw us looking around and asked us if this is where we slept when we were at sea, and how many of us there were. When we said twelve he whistled in astonishment and said something about sardines in a can. He then asked us if we'd wait there for ten minutes and he'd be back. True to his word he returned, and to our amazement he presented us with the contents of a hat he'd used to go round the rest of the shipyard workers and make a collection. He said something to the effect that they all hoped for our safety on future voyages. Hendricks and I were too overcome to do anything but stammer our thanks, to receive kindness like this from total strangers took our breath away. This was a prime example of the way we were treated by everyone we came into contact with in nineteen-forties New York.

As I've said before this all happened almost sixty years ago, and it's as vivid to me today as if it had occurred last week. The saddest thing of all to my mind is that over the intervening years I've seen that quality of compassion and kindliness gradually disappear from American life, to be replaced by an ugly, intolerant attitude to the rest of the world. My one fear is, that as most things American eventually cross the Atlantic, this may also blight our lives in Britain if it isn't resisted.

However, to get back to the story. We ended up being sent back to the hotel until further notice, and were met by the manager wearing an 'I told you so' expression on his face. He was entitled to his well-meant little gloat, which proved that he obviously knew someone who was working in the shipyard. In any event we were all delighted to be able to continue our most unexpected holiday. And this time Hendricks and I had almost eighty dollars between us from the whip-round on board, so we'd be able to buy some decent gifts for home, and some of the gear we'd been admiring in the shops.

And so we enjoyed another few days of our unexpected break wandering about and seeing something new every day. One of the highlights of those last days was our trip to see the liner *Normandie*, which had been the pride of the French merchant fleet and one of the most beautiful ships I'd ever seen. However, she was now lying on her side having capsized at her berth on pier eighty-eight in New York harbour. She had caught fire due to an accident with welding gear, or carelessness, or, as some quite knowledgeable people thought, sabotage. In any event, due to the amount of water pumped aboard by the fire fighters she'd snapped her mooring and simply rolled onto her side. To anyone who'd seen her in all her glory when she was the holder of the Blue Riband for the fastest crossing of the Atlantic it was heartbreaking to witness her now.

There were walkways built out to her, and we were allowed to walk out onto what had been her starboard side. What a sad ending to such a magnificent example of French maritime elegance. She had caught fire on the ninth of February nineteen-forty-two, and here we were seeing her now as simply so much rusty iron.

The American authorities who'd commandeered her as a foreign vessel of a hostile nation, Vichy France – had been in the process of turning her into a troopship when the fire broke out. With her speed and size she would have been a real asset to the allied war effort. However, it wasn't to be and she faced an ignominious end as scrap metal.

After these few extra days of holiday had ended we reluctantly packed our kit-bags once more, said our good-byes to all the people we'd come into contact with during our short, but wonderful stay at the Hotel Albert, and returned to the *Winchester* and reality. New York would soon be just a pleasant memory as new horizons appeared.

The ship was in a terrible state when we returned. Most of the deck timbers had been taken up on the fo'c'sle in order to secure the huge platform for the guns. All these timbers would have to be refashioned and laid to fit the new deck shape. Then all the seams would have to be caulked and sealed with pitch. It was obvious that we were going to make up for our short break by having to work from dawn to dusk getting the whole ship back to something resembling her former self.

So, with the bo's'n and the bo's'n's mates driving us on, we laid the new decking, painted everything, and did the hundred-and-one jobs necessary to make the ship seaworthy and presentable once more. In the evenings we were free to go ashore, but somehow we'd lost a lot of our initial enthusiasm by this time. Added to which we'd spent all our dollars, so at the end of our working day we were only too glad to simply get cleaned up and relax.

Looking back to those last few days ashore, I have a clear memory of one evening when we were walking somewhere near Times Square and saw a lot of people walking into what at first looked like a sort of chapel. Filled with curiosity we made enquires and found out it was a meeting to drum up support for the Soviet Union Solidarity Campaign. We were invited in, and once they knew who we were (i.e British seamen) we were treated to a wonderful evening. There were at least ten members of the American Communist Party present, and I had a great time explaining about our pre-war days, the *Local News Bulletin*, and Dad's struggles against bureaucratic officialdom. I remember thinking at the time, that working class aims are the same the world over. Simply a decent life, and an end to the dog-eat-dog attitude that dominated our society due to the greed of the few who hold the quality of our lives in their hands.

So for a few evenings after that our lack of dollars was not important. We met up with some of these sincere people, being invited to their homes and treated with the utmost kindness by some of the nicest people we'd met in all the time we were in New York. And I think I, in my own way, managed to paint a picture of what life was like for ordinary people in pre-war Britain, which was quite contrary to what they'd been led to believe.

The type of people I met in those far off days have all been silenced now. Anyone who espoused the doctrine of socialism has been ostracised and vilified by a powerful American elite who control the press so completely, that the American nation as a whole has been brainwashed against those they perceive as 'Pinko Liberals', but who in reality are simply kindly folk who, like me, believe that we are all entitled to a full and decent life, and not just crumbs from tables of the rich. Still, I'd better get back to my story, or the reader will be under the impression that I'm a believer in fair play, and not the survival of the fittest.

14

Back to the 'Old World'; and the War

So now, after a lot of hard work, we were ready to return to the war, and I must say the *Winchester* looked every inch the armed merchant vessel she now was, and ready for any eventuality she may be required to face.

The day came, and in keeping with the security ethos that prevailed then, we were woken at dawn and told to go to our mooring stations. With six of the fussy little New York tugs surrounding us we moved back to pier ninety once again. We were now to take on board about one thousand, five hundred American GI's plus all their equipment, and transport them to either Northern Ireland or the Clyde.

All shore leave had been cancelled, and so for this voyage at least that was the last we would see of New York. It had been an experience I would remember with pleasure for the rest of my life. I did correspond sporadically with one of the younger lads of the pro-soviet rallies. That was until nineteen forty-four when I received a last letter from his wife telling me he'd been killed somewhere in the Pacific after having been called up, or volunteering, for army service. Another sad loss of a life.

During the next three or four days we were kept busy loading supplies and taking the American troops on board. Until, at last fully laden, we were ready for the Atlantic crossing again. The difference this time, however, being that we were bringing fresh troops to Europe, and I'm sure that if Pearl Harbour hadn't taken place this would never have happened. The American attitude I believe would have remained the same as it was before this Japanese attack; namely, send plenty of supplies but remain neutral. So I suppose in its hideous way the Japanese attack had indirectly helped the allies at a time when we needed it most.

I remember thinking at the time how different these young soldiers were from the British troops we'd carried. Apart from the fact that their uniforms and general equipment were far superior to that issued to our boys, they seemed more confident. Their NCOs and officers seemed to treat them in a more humane manner than their British counterparts. There seemed to be a real sense of camaraderie between them. And when you stop to think about it that's the way it ought to be; after all, they were going to fight a common enemy. My feeling was that their's was – or so it seemed to me – a more egalitarian society without all our entrenched class divisions, and this showed in the rapport between the leaders and the led.

Finally we were ready to sail, and pier ninety was crowded with well-wishers. We were nosed out into the Hudson River by our flotilla of midget tugs until we came under our own power. Every craft on the river seemed to be there to say good-bye to us and these American lads. Ships' whistles were blowing and sirens howling in salute. It was very impressive, and I've often wished since that I'd had a camera, as that departure would have provided some really great pictures.

Our first destination would be Halifax in Canada to join the next east bound convoy. And Jerry, plus weather permitting, we'd soon be back in Blighty and enjoying a few days of home leave.

Two days later, after an uneventful trip along the American coast, we arrived in Halifax, Nova Scotia to find most of the convoy already there, probably having waited for us. There was a dozen or more ten thousand ton cargo ships; heavily laden by the look of them. But more ominously there were rather too many tankers. These were the rich targets that attracted the U-boats because their cargoes of oil were so vital to the war effort. And worse still, not only were the tankers and their cargo virtually irreplaceable, but with the oil being so inflammable and explosive very few, if any, of their crews ever survived a torpedo attack.

So after our arrival amid flurries of morse-code instructions and different hoisted signal flags, Convoy SC94 set sail from Canada in August 1942. And after much zig-zagging we settled into the usual pattern, with the convoy's speed dictated by the speed of the slowest vessel.

At that time of the year the nights were short and the daylight hours far too long, which meant that everyone from the captain down to the lowest crew member seemed to live in a state of anxiety. Our lookout duties were doubled, and we were put on four hour watches followed by four hours off. This only affected the deck hands, but was such a strain that after hours of staring out from the top lookout barrel high up on the foremast, every ripple began to look like a potential periscope. I devised my own method of relaxing by counting every ship in the convoy and hoping they'd all be there the next time I counted them.

Our first loss was a tanker. It happened on the second day out from Halifax at about 11pm when I was on watch high up on the foremast. I suppose we'd been lulled into a false sense of security by the quiet of the two previous days. The stricken tanker's end came almost as soon as the torpedo struck her. There was an enormous explosion followed by a mushroom of fire that lit up the whole convoy. She'd been carrying either aviation spirit or high octane, and simply disintegrated. She was gone with all hands in less than two minutes.

For a while there was chaos with the commodore ship morse-signalling a forty-five degree starboard turn. Destroyers from our escort party began dropping depth charges over the area where they'd located the U-boat by Asdic soundings. Three or four of the ships had miraculously avoided collisions in the dark and it took hours to get the convoy back into lanes again.

My lookout duty ended at midnight and after I'd exchanged places with my relief man I set off down the ladder. How I got down to the deck I don't know because I must have been suffering from delayed shock and was trembling from head to toe. I needn't have worried as our bo's'n, who was a thoughtful man, had been on a tour of the lookouts stationed at various vantage points along both sides of the ship – realising, I think, that the sinking of the tanker would have affected us all. He put an arm around my shoulder and gradually my legs stopped trembling and I became more composed.

We all went below to our mess-room and had a mug of tea before crawling into our bunks, fully clothed except for heavy watch coats and, of course, our kapok life jackets. This was a precaution we had to take due to the fact that after a torpedo hits a ship her lighting usually fails and there'd be no time to scramble about looking for your clothes.

I don't think any of us slept much that night, and it seemed no time at all until we were called at five thirty to go on lookout again. My watch was from six until ten in the morning but this time I was to spend my first two hours in the crow's-nest, some forty feet lower than the top barrel. This was a far more comfortable billet, and was connected to the bridge by a wind-up telephone; what technological delights we had in those days. Earlier on in the voyage I'd asked the chief officer if we could have a pair of binoculars permanently up in the crow's-nest to give us a further horizon. At that moment I knew how Oliver Twist must have felt when he asked for more gruel. The chief withered me with a look that said, binoculars were too technical for a sailor to comprehend. In any case, we didn't get any.

Once we'd had time to assess the sinking of the tanker, the common opinion seemed to be that she'd simply been attacked by an odd U-boat which had been lurking off the North American seaboard to catch any unwary ship, and that we'd left him too far astern – how wrong we were.

Our escort as far a Iceland consisted of an English cruiser in the lead position, with American destroyers patrolling up and down the outside of the convoy. Two days after this first casualty there was a sudden flurry of activity from the escorts on our port side. It seemed that their Asdic operators had detected something, and two destroyers were racing around trying to pinpoint whatever it was. It became apparent exactly what it was when there was another earsplitting explosion and another ship on our port side had been torpedoed. This time it was a ten thousand ton cargo vessel, probably loaded with vital supplies that would again be sorely missed. Fortunately this one took longer to go down, and a British corvette stood by her with no regard for its own safety, plucking many of her crew from what would have been almost certain death. Finally the ship seemed to settle with her bows in the air before slipping stern first to the bottom of the Atlantic.

That day we cursed every U-boat that had ever left Germany, and the 'heroes' who sailed in them to inflict this sort of cowardly savagery on decent sailors.

The whole convoy now turned ninety degrees to the south in order to present less of a broad target. This was all making our voyage home longer, but if we were to get home at all it was unavoidable. All that afternoon our escorts dropped patterns of depth charges, but they didn't seem to do a lot of good.

Darkness came and everyone on board our ship breathed a sigh of relief. We were bang in the centre lane of the convoy due to our vulnerability with so many troops on board. This made the poor devils in the outside lanes much more of a likely target for Jerry, and sure enough another tanker was torpedoed just before dawn the next morning. I didn't see this one go as I was off watch at the time, but according to my watch mates it was as horrific as the first one.

By this time we must have been somewhere to the south of Iceland, because our American destroyer escorts turned north to a base in Reykjavic, Iceland, and their duties were taken over by British Navy ships for the final half of the journey home.

We were beginning to realise that instead of being attacked by a lone U-boat, we had been stalked by a pack. And judging by the increased zig-zagging every few minutes there was nothing to be done except greater vigilance by our escorts and by ourselves as lookouts, then hope against hope that we'd slip past them into safer waters.

During the next few days we lost another two of the cargo ships in the convoy, making our total losses five. By this time I think everyone on our ship had become resigned to what was going on, and hoped that we'd get through without any more being sunk.

So far the weather had been reasonably mild, but we were now somewhere between Iceland and the North of Scotland and the glass (barometer) dropped like a stone. In hours we were in the middle of a south west gale, which was a blessing in disguise really because the seas became mountainous, putting paid to any further U-boat activity. However, it didn't do much for our lookout duties. Climbing up to the crow's-nest was bad enough under normal conditions, but was now a nightmare, with the ship rolling and pitching wildly, and of course all our heavy, bulky clothing. I had on more skins than an onion in order to keep warm at over a hundred feet above the deck, but I still got wet through.

We all cursed at the time, but we also knew that we couldn't relax our vigil for a moment. After our lookout watches were over we always had to report to the officer of the watch on the bridge, and any moans and groans I intended to make were quickly dispelled each time when I saw our skipper in his usual place in the corner of the wheel-house staring out at the heaving seas. He didn't seem to move, but I always knew he'd seen me report; he missed nothing.

At the time we'd left Halifax I'd seen him laughing and engaged in lively conversation with the pilot. Since then he seemed to have aged ten years. I don't think he'd actually left the bridge for days – or nights. I knew then what an awesome responsibility these old captains had in getting, or attempting to get, their ships from port to port with thousands of lives in their hands. He looked worn out and my respect for him grew enormously.

Fortunately there were no more sinkings, and in two days we were met by a destroyer fresh from the United Kingdom to escort us on the last leg of our journey. What a welcome sight that was.

One of the navy signalmen we had on board told us that a British corvette had sunk a U-boat. By what means we never found out, although there'd been a lot of depth charge activity before the weather had worsened. At least it was a little consolation for our own losses.

When dawn broke the following day we had land on both sides, and realised we were in the Irish Sea and obviously bound for the Clyde . . . We'd survived another voyage and lived to tell the tale.

We were in Glasgow once more, where we disembarked the Yankee troops and waited patiently to be paid off and sent home on leave. Here we were given a nasty shock, because now that the *Winchester Castle* had got increased fire power with her extra guns, she was being taken off troopship duties to become an assault ship. She was now almost a Royal Navy ship, and we, as her existing crew were to be offered what was known as 'T124' status, which meant, no matter how it was disguised by glib words, that we would then be Royal Navy personnel subject to every whim of naval officers, and no longer merchant seamen. There was no way I could accept this. I'd struggled too hard to become a merchant sailor to sacrifice it now.

To show how impressed we were by this turn of events the entire deck drew turned down the offer, as was our entitlement.

So we were all paid off, given rail vouchers, and because we were entitled to one day's leave for every month spent at sea, I was soon on my way to Barrow-in-Furness for eight days of very welcome leave.

I was sorry to leave the *Winchester* and the good friends I'd made, but that was the consequence of seagoing life, and I knew that after my leave I would be sent to the Shipping Pool, who in turn would send me to another ship.

15

A New Port of Departure

I arrived back in Barrow-in-Furness on September 8th 1942, as pleased to be home as my mother was to see me. I was looking forward to catching up on family and local news, and my mother to hearing the stories of my last voyage.

My homecoming was, however, tinged with a little sadness due to the fact that I wouldn't be going back to the *Winchester*. I had a lot of happy memories of her, and had met a grand crowd of shipmates who like me would all be going to new ships. I wondered often how many of us would survive the war, and I knew instinctively that the odds were against us. Yet I don't think any of us let it worry us unduly. At that age we had wings on our heels, and mishaps only happened to the other chap. Our philosophy was, 'take each day as it came'.

When once again my leave came to an end, I was in for another of the little surprises that cropped up in those turbulent times. Mr Garland of the shipping office sent me off away down south to Tilbury in Essex, which was a completely unknown area to me. Up until then I'd always sailed out of northern ports, which also meant on the whole with seamen from the North of England and Scotland. However, upon arriving on board the ship, I was pleasantly surprised to find two lads from Liverpool who I'd sailed with before, they'd just been sent down south like I had. Both of them were typical scousers, always ready with a humorous answer, and good shipmates into the bargain. This isn't going to be such a bad trip after all, I thought.

The ship was a nice looking vessel, with fast, rakish lines and somehow didn't have the look of a British tramp steamer. I soon found out why. She was a prize ship that had been boarded and captured in the Mediterranean by the British Navy in the first months of the war and taken to Gibraltar. She was, or had been, a German ship belonging to the cargo division of the Hamburg Amerika Line. Unfortunately, due to a lapse in security by the men guarding her in Gibraltar, some of her die-hard crew had sabotaged parts of her engine. It had taken until now to get her repaired and brought to Tilbury for her first cargo under the British Red Ensign.

Her present name was the *Caledonian Star*, though her original name had been the MV *Renate S. Muller*. The crew accommodation was aft and very impressive it was. As usual the deck crew were on the port side, and the engine-room personnel on the starboard. The captain and officers were all housed in the bridge centre-castle area. Each of us deck crew had a cabin to ourselves, which was an eye-opener to someone used to British ships. Typically on British vessels the crews were simply crammed into the odd spaces where nothing else could be stowed. This was obviously to maximise cargo space, and 'revenue'. Between the two sets of crew cabins aft was the galley, and a really nice crew dining-room-cum-lounge. Luxury indeed.

At the time of our joining the ship it was swarming with carpenters etc., from the dockyard, who were busy installing crash panels in all the cabin doors. It can be appreciated that all the doors on a ship have to be very substantial. Unfortunately, as a consequence, after any explosion caused by a torpedo or mine, or even by a ship to ship collision, if these doors jammed it was almost impossible for anyone inside to break out. Therefore these crash panels were to provide an escape route if this happened. They were about two feet by two feet six inches, made of soft wood and held in place by removable clips, thus enabling anyone trapped to at least get out of the cabin. What a boon these panels were, because one can only guess at how many poor seamen must have lost their lives jammed in their cabins as the ship sank before they were fitted.

While all this was going on, cargo was being loaded, and once we were all signed on ships articles it was left to us to familiarise ourselves with the ship. I spoke to one of the engineers who'd brought her from Gibraltar, and he told me that coming across the

Bay of Biscay the ship, sailing alone, had reached twenty-five knots. And added that now the engines had been repaired, because she had that sort of speed she would always be able to sail alone without the need for a convoy.

So a week after joining the ex-*Renate S Muller* we sailed from Tilbury – once more to an unknown destination. We cleared the English Channel and left Wolf Rock behind in daylight. As I recall, my first duty was on the fo'c'sle keeping lookout, and as we cleared the land I heard the bridge telegraph ring for maximum revs and full speed ahead.

After my lookout was over I was sent to 'stream the log'. As I explained earlier this is the device that is towed astern to show the distance covered. It is connected to a clock which records the actual mileage. It is this, together with dead reckoning, that helps to determine the ship's position each day. The second mate told me later that during those first twenty-four hours with a strong following wind the ship had covered six-hundred and twenty-five miles, making our average speed over twenty-six knots – what a greyhound of a ship.

Our course was mostly to the west, so it was obvious that we were headed for the USA. And six days after leaving Tilbury we entered Chesapeake Bay, Virginia, and were piloted into Newport News to discharge our cargo.

Now that America had entered the war the place was a hive of activity and our cargo was discharged in what seemed record time. The unloading carried on day and night and we were soon ready for the off again. At that time, unknown to us, the Germans had launched Operation Paukenschlag (Drumbeat). This was a plan to have U-boats lying off the eastern seaboard of the United States in order to wreak havoc among the ships leaving its many busy seaports en route for the large convoy bases such as Halifax, Nova Scotia, in Canada.

We left Newport News 'light ship' (no cargo) on the way to Philadelphia to load vital supplies for the United Kingdom. Alas we never got there. At four o'clock in the morning on the day after leaving Newport News Jerry pounced. Being so high out of the water we must have been a sitting duck, especially as we would have been silhouetted against the shore lights on our port side, there being no blackout in the USA at that time.

The explosion, when it came, was deafening. The only

fortunate thing was the fact that the 12am – 4am watch had just been relieved by the 4am – 8am watch so that most of us on board were still awake. Nevertheless, I personally was completely stunned, and for a little time lost the power of reason. Luckily, older and more experienced heads took charge of the situation and shepherded us to the lifeboats, by which time these had already been swung outboard and secured against the padded boom on the davits ready for lowering.

To me the next few hours after the torpedo struck were at best kaleidoscopic. I can remember some things vividly, but others are just blanked out. I've spoken to many others about the effect a torpedo attack had had on them, and heard different opinions. My younger brother, Jim, who was also torpedoed while serving on the destroyer HMS *Hurricane* in the Royal Navy, has given me one of the most succinct summaries I've heard. So I've included a letter below, that I received recently from him in which he outlined his thoughts on the subject. It also illustrates the difference between the non-stop emergency-training of the Royal Navy he was in, and the Merchant Service where I was, which being a civilian force got no such training whatsoever.

Dear Charlie,   *9/11/2001*

You once asked what were my reactions at the time of my torpedoing on HMS Hurricane, *and on reflection I think I may have given the impression that I was the bravest man since Captain Brown . . ? Not so, I've thought long and hard about those long-ago times, and I think an explanation is needed to clarify not only what my thoughts and actions were, but why I acted in the way I, and others, did at the time.*

I believe it goes back a long time to the way we all lived in deprivation in our childhood days. From your writings you always seem to have been very aware of the reasons for our poverty-stricken state, and able to see yourself in the scheme of things as they existed. However, this is a perception I never possessed at that time, or for many years afterwards. All I knew was that we had 'nowt'.

When I joined the Royal Navy I was given the first real clothes I ever remember as being mine alone. I was also fed on a regular basis, and was warm in a decent bunk at night.

I was at that time an ultra-royalist, and revelled in the training that we were put through on a daily basis. Every hour of every day we were instructed in how to behave in all circumstances; to obey the last command given without question by anyone of superior rank. And, of course, at that time 'everyone' was of superior rank to us young trainee matelots.

Square-bashing, rifle drill, running, climbing, knots and hitches, bends and splices, writing skills, in fact training of all kinds for twelve solid weeks. This was to get us used to 'obeying' without a flicker of resentment or question.

I, of course, enjoyed every second of it, as I was fulfilling my ambition to get back to sea again after my all too brief taste of it on board the MV Morgenan *— the Norwegian tanker that I had run away to sea on. Because of this I was always impatient to get back to sea, but the basic training seemed to take an eternity.*

Eventually, however, we got to sea and this is where the real training started. Every day we were drilled in lifeboat activity, gunnery, torpedo work, how to operate the depth charge throwing 'hedgehog' armaments, magazine loading and unloading etc., while at all times remembering that we were a warship and must be ready for action all around the clock. At any time of night or day 'Action Stations' would be sounded, and every member of the crew had an action station to get to fast, and carry out his duties. Duties which he'd had drummed into him time and time again until by the time action actually came it had become an automatic response to do what was required of him. So you see, when the Hurricane *was torpedoed bravery beyond the call of duty never came into it. We were really too trained, and too busy to do anything else.*

The same procedure applied when I was on HMS Wolfe *and the torpedo magazine and diesel room caught fire. Also on the occasion our torpedoes acted in strange ways after we'd worked on them to prepare them for use. They'd drilled it into us so much that when the time came it was all down to the training. This certainly stood us in good stead, because left to our own devices Adolf would have had it all his own way. Don't forget that we were all very young, naïve and apart from our training, quite thick.*

So there it is. No Victoria Cross stuff, just training. I hope these thoughts will help you to a better understanding of Hitler's part in my war. It was only after it was all over that I woke up to what you seem to have understood all along. I remember Dad saying to me when I got home, "Now you've fought for your country, Jimmy, which part of it's yours . . ?" I'm still waiting . . .

Jim

To continue with my own story:

The lifeboat I was assigned to had already been lowered into the water and was rising and falling on quite a heavy sea. One by one those of us still on board were slowly sent down a wooden ship-side ladder and the last man signalled the OK – two firemen had suffered leg injuries due to being caught between the ship's side and the lifeboat, but there was nothing we could do about it. We all rowed away from the sinking ship, but in the dark we didn't know in what direction we were going. Daylight couldn't come soon enough.

The seas were rough now, and a bitter easterly wind chilled us to the bone. We kept rowing in an attempt to keep warm, but we were soaked to the skin, and I think by this time the position we were in was beginning to dawn on us. If someone didn't spot us soon and effect a rescue we'd all die of hypothermia, or simply be washed out of the boat.

On that despondent note dawn came bringing daylight with it, and I then thought it had been better when it was dark. At least we hadn't been able to see the vastness of our surroundings. There was no sign of the ship or the other lifeboat, so we feared the worst. Luckily, however, our ordeal was soon to end. It must have been about mid-morning when we heard a distant ship's whistle, and the second mate, who was in charge of our lifeboat, fired a rocket. This was obviously seen, as minutes later an American coastguard cutter hove into view.

They decided that in the rough seas it would be too risky to try and come alongside, so they drifted a tow rope over to us and towed us slowly into the shelter of land where the sea was a bit calmer, and they were finally able to come alongside.

One by one the injured firemen were lifted aboard the cutter followed by the very grateful rest of us. We all huddled in the shelter of her bridge trying to keep out of the wind, and two hours later we were back in the harbour where we'd started from. Unfortunately, though, minus our ship. On reflection it seemed ironic that we'd captured her from the Germans, and the Germans had now sunk her. We obviously weren't meant to have that ship at all.

We were taken to the navy sick bay in Norfolk where we received the finest treatment possible. And after a hot shower and change of clothing, we all seemed none the worse for our ordeal. Good news came later that day when we learned that our other lifeboat had been found, and its occupants taken to somewhere further up the coast. This news was tinged by sadness, however, as we'd lost a junior engineer and two of the engine-room greasers. Also one of our firemen injured on leaving the ship had had to have a leg amputated. All this cast a cloud over our own survival, and frankly I wasn't too proud of my own performance. I can only assume that I must have been shocked into some kind of stunned semi-consciousness. Whatever the case I've never liked talking about it since, and quite frankly if my cousin hadn't convinced me to get it down as part of my memoirs it probably would have remained locked away at the back of my mind.

While we were in the sick bay in Norfolk, Virginia, we were told not to talk about a U-boat attack so close to the American coast. Obviously they believed that it might cause uproar if the people learned that even here Jerry could cause havoc.

Eventually we were all sent home to the UK under the terms of what was called DBS (Distressed British Seamen). At least we'd lived to sail another day.

Many years later, when sailing in a ship owned by the Everhard Company, we docked again in Tilbury. One evening I walked ashore to have a few pints at a pub which as far as I can remember was called The Theobald. However, during the evening I bumped into a chap who'd sailed on the *Caledonian Star* with me. He told me two interesting facts about the events of those days. One concerned the reason why there'd been so much hush-hush about our voyage to the States and the cargo we'd carried. Apparently (according to him) we'd had on board thousands of priceless paintings and artefacts, which were being shipped to the USA for safe keeping. I've often wondered if this was true or not. The second thing he told me was that the *Caledonian Star* (ex-*Renate S Muller*) had not actually been sunk by the torpedo, but had remained afloat half-submerged and drifting, creating a hazard to other shipping. Consequently she'd been sunk by gunfire in the 'deeps' off Virginia – salvage apparently not being feasible for various unspecified reasons.

16

From an Ocean Queen to a Coaster

Once again I found myself back in Barrow-in-Furness after what had been a pretty short but very eventful trip. Unfortunately, because of strict wartime secrecy regulations, those events could not be talked about, even to one's own family.

I was glad to find that my brother Jim was home at the time, having just returned from his 'running away to sea' venture on the MV *Morgenen,* and would shortly be joining the Royal Navy. How he'd hoodwinked the Royal Navy into accepting him I've no idea, for he was still well below the age to join up. Still, I couldn't say anything as I'd run off to sea myself, and I don't think entreaties of any sort would have dissuaded me or Jim.

On the last night of my leave Jim and I went on a pub crawl and finished up at a pub on the Strand in Barrow called The Ship. It was a place modelled on what a traditional English hostelry should be like; warm and friendly, welcoming and much frequented by the seagoing fraternity.

One room was out of bounds to the majority of us and this was known as the Captain's Room. Legend had it that when Barrow first became a notable port, as many as forty sailing ships would be moored bow first along the Strand, and their long jib booms, or bowsprits, would tower over the Ship Hotel. If any of the ships' captains could be induced to take a dram, which wouldn't take much inducement, this room was where they would sit and imbibe.

On the night that Jim and I were in, there was one grizzled old chap sitting in the Captain's Room with another younger man.

Both were obviously seamen, but we didn't pay them much attention. Little did I suspect that I was to meet them both again quite soon, in less congenial circumstances.

The following day a messenger arrived to ask me to go to the shipping office on the Strand to see Mr Garland. He was the man in charge of the allocation of seamen to ships requiring crews all over the UK. At that time I was very annoyed as I was entitled to eight days of leave, and now after only five of them I was being ordered to report for possible shipping out.

Annoyed or not I couldn't refuse. I'd heard of seamen being labelled cowards for refusing certain ships, and even though technically we were civilians the special powers act rendered us all part of the 'forces'. Apart from that we were duty bound, or morally bound, to do our best for our country, and if that meant sacrificing two or three days of leave it was unavoidable

Mr Garland was waiting for me when I arrived, and without further ado he told me to report to a coastal ship at the Buccleuch/Devonshire Docks at Vickers Armstrong's Shipyard. The ship, the *Kyle Fisher*, was due to sail on that evening's tide, but was short of an able seaman. He also stressed that its cargo was absolutely vital, but refused to elaborate. I remonstrated saying that I was a deep sea man, and not a coastal ship sailor. It was to no avail; the ship required an AB and as far as he was concerned that was that. So off I went to sign on to a ship that wasn't much bigger than one of the lifeboats on my previous ship.

As I walked over the High Level Bridge; the bridge that connected Barrow Island to the mainland of the Furness Peninsula, I could see the ship and wondered why Mr Garland had been so cagey about her cargo, because it was obvious to anyone crossing over the bridge that this was an enormous gun turret. The turret was sitting in the ship's hold with the two huge barrels protruding out over the ship's fo'c'sle and bows. There was certainly no mystery about this as they were obviously guns for some warship being built elsewhere. However, to see a little ship 'dwarfed' by her cargo like this seemed pretty incongruous to say the least.

I presented my pass at the shipyard gates, but had to sit twiddling my thumbs until a security man came to take me down to the ship. She was lying alongside in Devonshire Dock beneath a huge two hundred and fifty ton lifting capacity crane. This crane dominated the Barrow skyline at that time, and could be seen for miles. Apparently the only other one of its kind was in Newcastle.

I was taken on board and imagine my surprise when I came face to face with the two men I'd seen in the Ship Hotel the previous night. One was the skipper, Captain Crowther, who I was impressed with at first sight. He was typical of his kind, unassuming and yet supremely confident in his own ability to navigate a ship from one port to another successfully. I immediately thought, 'I'll bet he won't suffer fools gladly'. The other officer was the mate, or chief officer, and as he was the *only* officer I suppose he could have called himself the complete complement of the ship's officers, though somehow to me he didn't seem to fit any criteria for being a ship's officer in the first place. He spoke with a definite public school accent, and I could tell at once that he wasn't too keen on me. His whole attitude seemed to imply that he was slightly superior to all around him.

It transpired that he was the nephew of Sir John Fisher, the ship's owner. He had a decided limp, left over from some illness when he was a child, and a definite chip on his shoulder, caused I think by the fact that he had to mingle with the rest of us.

I was signed on in the ship's saloon and mentioned that Mr Garland, the shipping agent, had said it would only be for the one trip to deliver this vital cargo. Neither man answered, but I'm sure the mate was smirking at some joke of his own. I'm afraid the joke turned out to be on me, as the ship's articles had another four months to run, although I didn't find this out until later. This meant that I was contracted to the ship for another four months. It seemed that my pool officer, Mr Garland, had been less than truthful. Still, I would have to suffer it.

The mate, whose name was Barney Turner, told me to go and get my gear and report back at six o'clock for a seven o'clock sailing. From the start I knew there was going to be friction between us, and later I was proved correct. So off home I went to say my good-byes, collect my gear and join the three-hundred ton *Kyle Fisher*.

When I arrived back on board I received my first inkling that the mate was a nasty piece of work. The bo's'n met me to show me my bunk, and asked, "Where's your bedding?" I realised then that the mate had deliberately not told me that coastal ship's crew's had to supply their own blankets, etc., something I had never heard of. However, there was no time to worry about it as we had to go straight away to mooring stations and cast off to begin our trip from Devonshire Dock, through Buccleuch Dock into Ramsden Dock to await the full tide.

At high tide Ramsden Dock gates were opened and away we sailed down the Walney Channel and out into the Irish Sea. Watches were set which were four hours on and four hours off. I was put on the first watch, which meant eight o'clock until midnight, with a young ordinary seaman. The other watch was done by the bo's'n and the other able seaman. The four of us made up the whole of the deck crew.

At eight o'clock I had to take the wheel for what should have been a two-hour stint, followed by two hours on lookout. The officer on watch with me was the skipper, Captain Crowther, who seemed to be a pleasant and competent seaman. By this time we had rounded Walney Island and were heading to sail north up the Irish Sea between the Mull of Galloway and Northern Ireland. The weather, as I remember, was windy and there was quite a fair sea running.

Apart from telling me of any course corrections while I was at the wheel the skipper never spoke for almost an hour, and I remember thinking, 'this is going to be some voyage: A captain who doesn't speak, and a mate who has taken a dislike to me for some unknown reason.'

I was watching the compass repeater to make sure I didn't stray off course when the skipper suddenly turned to me out of the blue and said, "I believe you weren't told to bring some bedding on board." I told him this was true, and he said, "Don't worry, son, you'll have blankets by the end of your watch." How he'd found out I don't know, but I thought, 'at least I'll not be cold off watch.' He then said, "Oh! by the way, you're a fine helmsman. I've been watching you."

"Thank you very much," I replied, and told him of my spell as a quartermaster on the *Winchester Castle,* which I'd detested, but that this was altogether a more relaxing type of wheel-house, and that the gyrocompass was a great improvement on the normal ship's compass in its binnacle that I'd been taught on.

By this time my two-hour spell was over and the ordinary seaman was due to take over. But where was he? He'd been out on the wing of the bridge on lookout, but had now vanished.

f

There was a simple explanation. It seemed he'd never steered a ship before, and had just panicked as his turn at the wheel grew nearer. Captain Crowther found him in the galley frightened to death at what would happen to him. The skipper kindly put him at his ease and told him to make two mugs of tea and bring them up to the wheel-house. For the next two hours I had to coach him and stand with him while he attempted to learn to steer. Unfortunately he had no natural flair for it, and I remember thinking that I'd be doing most of the steering on our watch from now on. I hoped he'd improve, but didn't expect too much.

At about ten minutes before midnight the mate came up to the bridge to relieve the captain and take the twelve o'clock to four o'clock watch. The skipper asked him if he'd had a good sleep, and if he'd been warm enough. The mate looked quite puzzled but answered yes to both questions. The skipper said, "Good!" then asked him how many blankets he'd had on his bunk. The mate answered that he had three. The skipper then said, "That's all right, then. You won't miss two, so go down to your cabin and bring them up to the wheel-house. You allowed this seamen to join the ship without explaining to him that bedding was not provided, so it's only fair that you should make sure he's warm enough when he's off watch."

The mate gave me a poisonous look, but did what he was told.

This, then, was my first experience of sailing on a small coastal vessel. The skipper and I had hit it off, but Barney Turner, the mate, was a different type altogether and it looked as though he and I were going to be at loggerheads from now on. All I could do was keep my counsel and make sure my work was up to scratch. That way he'd have no room to complain.

So the voyage entered a sort of fitful monotony during daylight hours, even though the weather was poor things weren't too bad. Sailing through the Sound of Islay, one of the Hebridean Islands, was a stunning experience. The channel between Islay and Jura was so narrow that I felt as if I could almost touch the land on either side.

We sailed on up between the westernmost point of the Island of Skye and North and South Uist into the Minch. It was at this point, four days out from Barrow, that we ran into a north westerly gale of force eight and for about twenty-four hours we stood off from the Scottish mainland almost at a standstill. We were due to navigate through the Pentland Firth, which was the channel between the North of Scotland and the Orkney Islands, but daren't attempt it while the wind was so fierce. The tide there ebbed and flowed between the North Sea and the Atlantic, sometimes at almost eight or nine knots. From Cape Wrath on the western tip of Scotland to Duncansby Head on the eastern tip is approximately seventy miles, and can be one of the most treacherous stretches of water around the British Isles.

During this period the ship was doing everything but turn over. The skipper kept the ship's head directly into the wind, because with our top-heavy cargo it would have been criminal to risk rolling from port to starboard. The seas were breaking over the bow and everything forward of the bridge was under water. To make matters worse my opposite number, the ordinary seaman, had become violently ill with seasickness and was confined to his bunk. Consequently my whole watch was spent at the wheel, so as you can imagine I was delighted with life in general!

After two days of this I was completely tired out. It was like being on a roller-coaster, with the added misery of being cold and wet through. The constant four hours on and four off left one slightly disorientated to say the least. It was almost a week since we'd sailed from Barrow, and we were only about a third of the way to our destination at Newcastle. I swore at that time that, if possible, when my time on this bouncing bucket ended, I'd try to sail only on ships of a decent size, and preferably to the tropics.

Gradually, though, the weather eased and we were able to round Cape Wrath and commence our trip through the Pentland Firth. By this time the skipper was almost grey with fatigue, and it was only by sheer will power that he was able to keep awake. I never knew how old he was, but he must have been about sixty in my opinion. He hadn't left the bridge since the storm began seventy-two hours before, and I realised then that he really had no one to turn to for support. The mate, Barney Turner, seemed to have a good grasp of his job as far as the running of the ship was concerned, but in my opinion he hadn't the quality of command necessary to be able to act in an emergency; such as the one we'd just been through.

During the long hours on the wheel the skipper and I had formed a rapport and I knew he trusted my steering. So when, after my first two hours, I was relieved by the bo's'n to have a hot drink and a smoke down in the warm galley, I took the opportunity as I went below to knock at the mate's cabin door. I then told him that the captain was almost all in, and if he agreed I would stay on watch with him until the captain had a few hours sleep. In this way, with four of us on watch he'd be able to relax. The mate agreed at once, so I had my half hour break and reported back to the wheel-house.

Barney was already there and had explained to the skipper what had been agreed. The old chap didn't need forcing, he gave a list of courses to follow to steer through the Firth and jokingly said, "Don't run into the Old Man of Hoy." So off he went for some well earned rest, leaving Barney in command with two good lookouts and myself at the wheel.

Everything went smoothly during that long night except for one incident that is worth mentioning. I had done my two hours at the wheel, and was then out on the wing of the bridge on lookout for a two hour spell when I 'sensed' rather than saw another vessel approaching at high speed. Of course, being wartime she carried no lights, and in the blackness I could see nothing.

I slid the wheel-house door open and called the mate out. By this time we could hear the bump, bump, of either her engines or propellers. There was nothing to be done, we simply stood there peering out over the side. And then although we saw nothing she went past our port side and I don't think there was more than ten feet between us. Barney hazarded a guess that it was a destroyer travelling at speed. All in all we'd had a narrow escape, and were rather glad it wasn't daylight for perhaps then we might have done something silly and made matters worse.

So that long night ended, and as dawn came we could see Duncansby Head on our starboard beam, and would soon have to change course down E-boat Alley, as the North sea between Great Britain and the Continent had come to be known.

At about 7am the skipper arrived back on the bridge and he looked a new man after his rest. He then set course for our next port of call which was Methil in the Firth of Forth. Methil had become a convoy base for the traffic of small ships in the North Sea. Our escorts were usually ex-trawlers commandeered by the navy, or sometimes very fast MTBs (motor torpedo boats), which although not as fast as the German E-boats, still gave us a feeling of security.

We arrived at Methil some eleven days after leaving Barrow, and anchored offshore to be fitted with a small barrage balloon before our final leg south. The theory was that it would deter any dive-bombers who would risk snagging on the balloon cable if they attacked us. Whether it would have been effective in practice or not I don't know as fortunately we were never dive-bombed. However, it did give us some sense of protection.

We were anchored off-shore for two days, during which time our convoy of about ten coastal colliers gathered, and away we went again, hopefully to our final destination, Newcastle-upon-Tyne. I thought at the time, and said as much to the mate, if Jerry doesn't see the convoy itself, the sight of ten balloons making their way south would be a dead give away, and must have been visible for miles. Still, we came to no harm on that trip.

During the course of the last two weeks the mate and I had reached a sort of mutual understanding, and the initial antagonism he'd displayed when we first met seemed to have diminished. But even the captain never called him Barney, always Mr Mate, so I followed the skipper's example and respected the formalities. After all, he was the ship's chief officer, so I grudgingly always called him Chief.

He seemed to be in the process of growing a beard, but as yet it was a wispy affair and rather untidy. To make conversation one night I asked him if he was growing a beard purposely – because frankly it didn't suit him at all, though I was too discreet to say that. His answer quite surprised me, simply because I couldn't picture him in any other surroundings apart from the ship. It seemed he was getting married in the next few months, and had only one razor blade left for the happy day. At that time of three-hole safety razors, blades were very difficult to obtain; all steel stocks going to the war effort.

During my last trip to New York I'd bought a 'Schick' injection razor, which was an innovation far ahead of its time. It comprised an ordinary type of safety razor combined with a sort of magazine of spare blades. After shaving, the used blade was ejected by the insertion of the magazine into a slot on the razor, while at the same time it deposited a new blade ready for use again. I told the chief that he could borrow it at any time he wanted as I had plenty of spare blades. I think that this cemented our rapport, and afterwards we got on quite well. A small ship like this was no place for acrimony.

We finally docked under the big crane at Newcastle nearly three weeks after we'd left Barrow, and delivered our gun turret cargo safe and sound. I must admit that during the storm en route I'd had my doubts that these particular guns would ever fire a shot in anger.

After we'd discharged the gun turret and barrels we moved to another berth down river to await our next orders, but my own priority was to try to get the skipper to pay me off so that I could get back to deep sea sailing. So, taking the bull by the horns, I approached him determinedly, asking him to pay me off and giving my reasons. As I've said before, he was a kindly old chap normally, but on this occasion I must have caught him at a bad time. He'd just returned from a visit to the ship's agents ashore, and when I knocked at his saloon door he opened it with a face like thunder. He listened to my request in silence, and when I'd finished my little speech he said, "If that's what you're wasting my time with the answer is no. The ship's articles are due to run until the end of February 1943, so until then I'm afraid you'll have to put up with a small ship."

There was nothing more to be said, and as I had no real friend aboard who I had any time for, I decided to go ashore and drown my disappointment alone. Even this was a let down, because I was so tired after the constant four hours on and four hours off that I almost fell asleep over my pint. In the end I decided that my situation wouldn't be altered in a glass, so my best plan would be to accept the skipper's words and make the most of it. It was the only choice I had.

The next day, refreshed by about ten hours sleep, things took on a less dire aspect, and I remember thinking that in two months time it would be Christmas, and we may even get a bit of home leave.

The reason for the Skipper's foul mood the previous day was explained to me by the mate that morning. Apparently two new ships were being built in Vickers Armstrong's shipyard in Barrow for the coastal trade, and whilst our ship owners, J. Fishers, would not actually own them they would be managing them on behalf of the government. If they survived the war the ownership would then pass to J. Fishers. The shore supervisor for the company was a Mr Percival who in my opinion was a thoroughly nasty piece of work, who used his position of power as an extension of his normal bullying nature.

In those days James Fisher & Sons had their offices on the Stand in Barrow, and were also the consuls to the Royal Dutch Government. In their heyday they had owned forty or so sailing ships and had been quite a presence in the shipping world. Between the wars, however, their fortunes had waned somewhat until by the outbreak of the war they only had about eight small coasters left. As soon as war was declared, of course, they were once more in great demand. This change in the company's fortunes had obviously gone to Mr Percival's head, and one would have thought he was supervising the Cunard White Star Line. However, what had upset our captain was the fact that he had been offered the command of one of the new ships, but Percival had now reneged on this. No wonder our skipper was upset.

Personally, at the time I couldn't resist a slight smile at his discomfiture. He'd jumped down my throat when I'd asked him to sign me off to go to a bigger ship, and now he was landed with a similar problem. At least I had only a few months to go, whereas he was stuck there for as long as Mr Percival decided.

Our sailing orders finally came and we were to sail to somewhere still unknown the following day. As we were sailing 'light ship', in other words without cargo or ballast of any kind, we were allowed to sail alone and without our obligatory barrage balloon to give our position away to hostile eyes. The captain was on the bridge as we left Newcastle and sailed down the River Tyne, and thankfully he was in a much better mood now that he'd come to terms with his disappointment over the new ship.

As we approached North Shields a pilot cutter came out to meet us with a naval officer on board. He'd brought our sealed orders for the next port of call and details of the probable cargo. He departed, wishing us a safe voyage, and left the captain in his saloon studying the orders, and the rest of us wondering if we'd turn to port for the north or starboard for the south. As we left the Tyne he arrived back on the bridge and gave me the new course to steer. It turned out to be starboard for the south, and that our next stop was to be Chatham on the River Medway. Chatham was essentially a Naval port, so whatever we were going there for had to be connected with the Royal Navy. We could only wait and see.

As we left the mouth of the Tyne and sailed into the North Sea the weather suddenly worsened, and I remember thinking, 'Here we go again! This is going to be the normal state of the weather now that winter's approaching. What a prospect to look forward to.'

The wind was from the south-east, about force seven or eight and blowing as cold as charity. I was relieved on the wheel by the next watch, and the mate was waiting for me to go forward with him to check every wedge that held the hatch-cover tarpaulins in place. In those days, long before metal hatch covers were even thought of, the ship's cargo holds were sealed and made sea-proof (hopefully) by wooden hatch covers which were supported on huge girder-like cross beams, with the whole thing being covered by thick canvas tarpaulins. These tarpaulins were secured by batten irons and wooden wedges driven into cleats around the sides of the hatch combings. Checking them was a tedious procedure, but vital when one's life depended on preventing the sea from flooding into the cargo holds. The mate and I checked, and checked again, until finally there was nothing more to be done.

Our last job was to rig two life-lines from below the bridge to the fo'c'sle head in case we needed to inspect them again. By this time there was a heavy sea running and the mate and I were wet through from the spray. We were more than glad to call it a day and go to dry out with a hot drink in the warmth of our quarters.

The weather was getting worse by the minute, and it looked as though we were in for a full blown gale. Meantime my watch-mate, the ordinary seaman, had succumbed to sea sickness once more, which meant me doing four hours at the wheel again. It crossed my mind then that he was in the wrong profession if every time the weather turned he had to retire to his bunk.

I think at this point I would like to explain what a violent storm at sea is like, particularly on a small ship such as this one. Gale force winds and foul weather on land are bad enough and cause a lot of damage to buildings etc., as well as disrupting normal life to a degree. However, in contrast such gales at sea become a matter of life and death, and that is no exaggeration. One wrong order on the bridge, or even an order badly carried out can result in a ship foundering and all on board being lost. Nine times out of ten in such cases there isn't time to launch a lifeboat, and of course it's only in recent years that determined efforts have been made to improve the life-saving capabilities on board ordinary merchant ships. Such things as survival suits and inflatable life rafts were never even thought of in those days.

As we ploughed on south it became clear that we should have stayed in the shelter of the River Tyne. It was now nearing dusk, and it was obvious that we daren't attempt a turn, because if the wind and sea had hit us sideways on we would have been turned over in minutes. All we could do was keep our bow directly into the teeth of the gale, and if the chance presented itself run for shelter somewhere down the coast. The little ship was now digging her bow deep into the seas and everything forward of the bridge was submerged under water. I was certainly thankful we'd checked the hatch covers. Slowly with each heavy sea she would raise her bow and half her length clear of the sea until she seemed to be standing on her stern. We began to fear that if this carried on much longer she would eventually go under altogether.

Moving about on board had become a nightmare. The ship was making no progress forward at all, in fact, if anything we were losing ground. On instructions from the mate I'd attempted to 'stream the log' to get some indication of how far we'd travelled. But to be affective in registering the mileage on the clock, the rotor on the end of the log line had to be towed in the ship's wake, and as we weren't moving forward at all the attempt was pointless.

No one on board had had any rest since leaving Newcastle because it was a waste of time trying to lie in a bunk. Even simply moving about was like being on a roller coaster, with the added disadvantage of having to try and do all the mundane jobs essential to the running of a ship. At midnight it was time for me to relieve the other watch and I wasn't looking forward to four hours on the wheel with no relief, due to the fact that my watch-mate was still lying comatose.

I took over the wheel from the other watch and only then, looking out at the sea through the clear spinning, circular glass panel in the window, did I realise just how bad the weather was. Steering was simply a matter of keeping an eye on the compass and at the same time on the sea breaking against the bow. I tried to anticipate each wave before it struck and to compensate by steering into it. If a wave knocked us off course it was minutes before the ship could be brought back.

The skipper was on watch with me, and the only order he gave was to steer according to the sea and not to take too much notice of the compass. He knew that I understood what he meant; i.e. that our only course of action was to keep the ship on the best heading to ride out the storm without coming to any harm. At this point I said a silent thank you to the Norwegian lads who'd taught me to steer on my first ship.

I needn't have worried about it being a long four hours, I was too occupied to notice the time passing. In fact, I was surprised when the mate and the next watch arrived on the bridge. I was tired out and glad to stagger below to my bunk. I thought that with all the violent movements of the ship I'd never sleep. However, it was as if I'd been pole-axed, and clinging onto the bunk rails I slept like a log for three and a half hours, right until it was time to go on watch again. I don't know how, but I felt almost fully refreshed as I went to report to the bridge. I had all of my cold weather gear on, and over that an oilskin coat and sou'-wester hat, otherwise by the time I'd reached the wheel-house I'd have been soaking wet, through having to negotiate the open deck. The weather didn't seem to be improving, but at least now that it was daylight things didn't look quite so ominous.

I think, looking back to that time, it was the first occasion I'd ever had misgivings about a life at sea. Whether it was the demoralising effect of four hours on and four hours off I don't know, but I felt fed up to the back teeth. I was also dispirited by the thought that I would have to put up with it until the end of February the next year, when hopefully my contract would end, and I'd be able to find a larger ship – preferably sailing to somewhere warm.

Halfway through my watch the wind swung round to the east, almost east by north. The skipper shot out of the wheel-house on the weather side realising, I think, that this was the break we'd been waiting for. He seemed to sniff the air for a few minutes like a gun dog scenting prey. What a faculty these old ship's masters had for knowing the weather. He came back into the wheel-house and first blew down the voice pipe to the engine-room. He explained to the engineer that when he rang the telegraph for full speed he meant exactly that, and a bit more. It was my turn next.

"Do exactly what I tell you to do as soon as I signal," he said. He then put his head out of the wheel-house again; came back and gave two rings for full speed. He waited until he could feel the increased vibration from the engine, and quietly told me to steer to starboard and due west, and then hold that course. As I followed his instructions the wind and seas were soon behind us, and the sickening, violent motion of before lessened considerably.

Two hours later we entered the mouth of the River Humber and found a decent, sheltered anchorage where we were to stay for the next two days until the storm ended, and we were able to continue to Chatham.

I've tried to paint a picture of the effect of a violent storm at sea on a small ship. If my description sounds a little melodramatic believe me it doesn't tell the whole story at all. I think that from the skipper downwards none of us really believed we'd weather it. Thankfully we did, but sadly we heard later that a converted trawler/patrol boat had sunk with all hands during the storm. Tragedy for some, salvation for others. Once again I thought of the song, *No Roses Bloom On a Sailor's Tomb*.

And so the weeks passed on. We 'tramped' from one port to another with various cargoes, but suffered no more weather as severe as I've just described.

I finally paid off the *Kyle Fisher* at the end of February 1943, and I can't honestly say I had any regrets. I was sorry to say good-bye to old Captain Crowther, who had turned out to be a man to respect. And after our first unfortunate encounter I'd also come to like Barney Turner the chief officer (mate). But overwhelmingly I was delighted to be finished with this type of coastline sailing, at least for the present . . . What a blessing we can't see into the future.

And so it was home at last to Barrow for a few days' leave. Jim had left and gone into the Royal Navy now and was training as a torpedo man. Where Bill was I didn't know, but Mam was delighted to have at least one of us home for a while, and I intended to really enjoy a decent rest in a bed that didn't move.

So here I was at home again. I was due six days of leave and I was determined to enjoy them, so instead of depending on the Barrow shipping office to find my next ship I decided to ask for a transfer to either Glasgow or Liverpool. These two ports were

131

where nearly all the deep sea ships were sailing from, and I was adamant that I was not going to be caught out again. I'd had enough of the British coast for a while.

However, I found that this was a strange moment in the war for me, though possibly other servicemen went through the same experience. Here I was in Barrow-in-Furness, my home town, for what I considered a well earned break, and yet I was lonely and fed up. And to be honest I wanted to get back to sea.

The reason was, I think, that I now knew no one in Barrow sufficiently well to call them a friend. Most of my contemporaries from school days, and the lads I'd grown up with from the Hindpool district, were either away in one or other of the forces, or in reserved occupations such as Vickers Armstrong's Shipyard – I suppose that being a skilled fitter was of more help to the war effort, indirectly, than if they'd been sent off to carry a rifle or crew a ship. The trouble was that the ones in reserved occupations seemed strangely reluctant to mix. I've realised since that this was probably through a combination of resentment that they were stuck in the shipyard and guilt that they weren't in the forces doing what they thought of as their proper 'bit' for the country. Of course, they had no control over the situation, but I think this was almost certainly the reason they didn't want to socialise with us lads on active service. It probably made them feel as though they were dodging service, when in reality they had no choice.

So after five days I'd had enough, and explained to Mam what I intended to do. She was too understanding to try and dissuade me, so off I went to see old Mr Garland, our shipping master. He was quite amenable when I explained that I wanted to go to Glasgow or Liverpool in order to get on a decent sized ship, and he issued me with a travel voucher for Glasgow without a quibble. He wished me well and off I went.

17

The Middle East
Beckons Again

I said my good-byes the following day and took the train for Glasgow, hoping I would soon be shipped out. Each day I had to attend the shipping pool on James Watt Street, while I was living at the Sailors' Home round the corner on the Broomilaw.

Glasgow was a very cosmopolitan city during those war years. To walk down Argyle Street was an eye-opener. The Clyde had become the hub of all the Atlantic shipping and the Clyde Estuary, or The Tail of The Bank, as it was known, was the main convoy base for shipping most of the supplies and men to all the various theatres of war. The logistics for these supplies must have required an amazing amount of planning and co-ordination: although Murphy's Law was evident sometimes. I was told that after one particular bout of pilfering from cargoes being sent overseas, some bright boffin with a cargo of boots to ship, decided to stop this by sending all the right-foot boots on one ship and all the left-foot boots on another, to be reunited only at their destination. Unfortunately that's where Murphy's Law stepped in. The ship carrying the right-foot boots was torpedoed and sunk, causing some wag to remark that if the Eighth Army were to defeat Rommel they'd have to 'hop' to it . . . This joke, of course, would have been lost on the poor lads who'd gone down with the ship.

As I said earlier, Glasgow was a very colourful place at that time. Uniforms of every army and navy belonging to the allies could be seen on any walk through the city. I often came across ex-shipmates waiting as I was for another ship. When this happened we'd retire to the nearest hostelry and have a good chinwag about our experiences since we'd sailed together, and also raise a glass to the lads who'd sail no more.

I think I'd waited almost a week before I was given my sailing orders. A full crew was required for a ship which at that time was somewhere abroad. We were all to be sent out as passengers to relieve the crew whose service contract had expired. We were therefore given the rest of that day off to do our last minute shopping, write letters home etc.

The next day we all travelled to Gourock to board the ship which was to take us overseas to join the one we'd been assigned to. At Gourock we were ferried out to the ship and to my astonishment I found that it was the *Llanstephan Castle*, which I'd sailed on previously. So after we'd been shown our living quarters and settled in I decided to see if any of the crew who'd been on board with me were still there. I discovered that there were a few, but unfortunately they weren't people I'd known particularly well. The bo's'n was still there, but he'd been an ignorant bully so I ignored him. Also on board, and still an ordinary seaman, was the Irish lad who'd joined my first ship with me in Barrow. We chatted for a while, but he didn't seem a very happy lad at all, so as soon as I could I said cheerio and went back to my cabin, thinking I'd better just let sleeping dogs lie.

Once again there came the old familiar routine of flags being hoisted to pass instructions from the commodore ship, plus Aldis lamps flashing messages in morse code, and soon we were all formed up into a convoy for another voyage into the unknown. It was now the beginning of March 1943, and while the heavy losses of ships and seamen had eased somewhat, every precaution was still being taken to minimise the danger from the 'underwater assassins' in U-boats.

As we got under way, even though we were zig-zagging and using other evasive tactics, it soon became evident that we were heading south. From my point of view it was a unique experience to now be a passenger, and have no duties at all on a ship that I'd once crewed.

As the weather improved the further south we got, it was a pleasure just to be able to laze about in the sun and only go below at meal-times. A spirited and enjoyable 'crossing the line'

134

ceremony at the Equator made a welcome break for all the troops going overseas for the first time. I couldn't help wondering, though, how many of them would be coming back when the war was over.

After an uneventful passage from the Clyde, we arrived at Cape Town, South Africa, still no wiser as to our final destination, or even what kind of ship we would find when we got there. However, this wasn't a problem at that moment; here we were in Cape Town and may as well enjoy our stay. I even decided that I may possibly be persuaded to sample a tot or two of the celebrated 'Cape Brandy' – purely for medicinal purposes, of course.

We were housed for three days in a hotel just off Alderly Street, which was at that time the main street, and had an enjoyable time before being told to pack our bags and make our way to the main railway station. We were being taken overland to Durban in Natal Province: a journey of almost three days by train.

To say the least I was as pleased as punch, in fact I think we were all looking forward to the prospect of crossing Africa in style. Our accommodation consisted of narrow, but very comfortable two berth compartments. The beds were folded up during the day, with the lower one becoming a seat. I spent hours looking out at the scenery, though once we'd left the Cape behind it was mostly open veldt. But what a profusion of wildlife. wildebeest and springboks were in preponderance, but with the occasional herd of elephant and zebra here and there.

Our meals were served in a long restaurant car and were really excellent. I suppose most of the food must have been pre-cooked and reheated as required. We stopped occasionally at small halts in order to stock up on coal and water for the locomotive, and I remember our stop at Ladysmith particularly well. We were allowed four hours to leave the station and have a good look around. There was a little monument in the square outside the station and I wasn't too sure at the time what it was for, but I realised later that it must have had something to do with the famous siege that took place there during the Boer War. I couldn't help noticing, however, that there was a marked reluctance on the part of the townsfolk to engage in any sort of conversation. None of us thought too much of it at the time, but simply enjoyed the chance to stretch our legs.

We next stopped at a place called Bethlehem, and here we found out why the people of this province, the Transvaal, weren't keen on us. This area was apparently the heartland of the Ossawa Bront Veg, a Boer organisation that was in sympathy with the Germans, due to their Dutch origins, and to the fact that since the Boer War they'd simply hated the British, looking upon South Africa as their rightful domain. Every time we'd attempt to ask them questions they'd immediately revert to speaking Afrikaans and ignore us. It seems that at the outbreak of the war this pro-German organisation had held anti-British rallies, trying to persuade the government of Africa to join Hitler and refuse the allies any right to use their ports.

Fortunately for us the prime minister of the time, Jan Smuts: affectionately known as 'Slim Jannie' – who incidentally had fought against us in the Boer War as a general, and very effectively too – was a realist. He knew that with both Russia and the United States involved on our side, it was in South Africa's interests to join the allies, since it was only a matter of time before we won. As a result most of the leaders of the Ossawa Bront Veg were imprisoned until the end of hostilities.

Leaving the Orange Free State behind we then crossed the Drakensberg Mountains, and in glorious sunshine finished our journey in Durban, Natal Province. It had been a fascinating trip, but now it was back to wondering where we would go next.

On leaving the train we were taken to a large warehouse type building on the Durban dockside at a place called Maydon's Wharf. It had been fitted out with a dining area and large dormitories. It was quite comfortable, and it seemed that we were to stay here until further orders arrived. I buttonholed one of our officers the next day and asked him what all the mystery was about. He said he'd only found out himself the day before. It appeared that the ship we were joining was waiting at anchor in Alexandria harbour, Egypt. He insisted that was all he knew, so I had to accept his word for it. At least we now knew where we were bound, though we still had no idea what kind of ship we'd find there.

We were in the warehouse for a week, until a large passenger ship tied up at the wharf. She was the *Regina Del Pacifico* (Queen of the Pacific). She belonged to the Royal Mail Shipping Company, and had now been turned into a troopship. In peacetime, and before she'd been bought by the Royal Mail Company, she'd belonged to the Pacific Steam Navigation Company and had been the pride of their fleet sailing to the South Americas. She was a lovely vessel, and even painted in her drab, grey wartime colours was still a fine looking ship. We learned that she was to take us to the Port of Suez (Port Taufiq), from where we were to go by rail once more to Alexandria via Cairo.

The ship embarked about a thousand troops, and once they and all their equipment were on board we were next. We were crammed, about a hundred of us, into a space that would have been crowded with half that number. We has trestle tables for eating during the day, but they had to be folded away at night. Each man was given a mattress and a blanket for night time, and even though it was crowded I had to admit that I'd had worse conditions during my few short years at sea. The weather was good, so at least we'd be able to get up on deck for fresh air.

Eventually we set sail on what was to be the last leg of our journey to Egypt. As we sailed out of Durban and past the Bluff the Lady in White didn't disappoint us. There she was singing us on our way as usual, and I must say bringing a special lump to our throats with *Land of Hope and Glory*. I found that she'd now increased her repertoire by adding a beautiful old Voortreker song, *Sari Marais*, for the South African lads. To quote an old show business saying, 'there wasn't a dry eye in the house'. I was actually glad when her voice faded into the distance as I found it too upsetting. A silence had fallen over the ship with everyone wrapped up in his own thoughts.

However, our spirits were too high to dwell on sad things for long: and in any case the tannoy soon announced that lunch was ready for our section, so off we all trooped below to eat. One outstanding thing about that voyage on the *Regina Del Pacifico* was the food. How the ship's cooks and bakers did it under what must have been immense stress and strain I don't know. They were catering for almost two thousand hungry mouths three times a day, and the standard they set was amazing to say the least.

After two or three days of this idle sailing I was bored stiff. I made a poor passenger as I was too interested in what makes a ship tick. Fortunately, as we had the run of the entire ship I explored those areas where my counterparts, the deck crew, were working. I came across a few of them painting the superstructure on the boat deck one day, and was having a good chat about all the things seamen talk about; previous ships and experiences etc., when the bo's'n appeared. He was what is known as a 'company man'. In other words he only ever sailed on ships belonging to one shipping line. This was known as being 'established', while those of us who went from one company to another were known as 'unestablished'. Each of these arrangements had their advantages, but personally I preferred to be able to go from one type of ship to another. He seemed a decent sort of bloke, and after telling him who I was and how bored I was becoming he asked me if I was able to splice large manilla or sisal ropes, and also if I could splice mooring wires. When I said I could, he asked me if, being so at a loose end, I'd mind teaching these skills to some of the younger deck crew. He emphasised that there'd be no money for doing it, but he promised a couple of tins of cigarettes for my trouble. So for the next week I had a class of lads all willing to learn, while the bo's'n, shrewd as they come, got all his snapped mooring ropes re-spliced at next to no cost. Still, it had passed the time on nicely for me, and I was also glad of the fags. To be quite honest it was something of an ego trip.

Finally we arrived in Port Taufiq at the eastern end of the Suez Canal and began disembarking for our final journey overland to Alexandria.

After waiting on the quayside for a long time in sweltering heat we were met by an agent of Thomas Cook's. It seemed a bit incongruous in the middle of a war to be greeted by the agent of a travel firm. He was British, so I suppose he must have been trapped in Egypt when war was declared and simply carried on.

He had arranged an overnight stay for us in Suez at the Paris Hotel, but any resemblance to the French capital ended at the name. Obviously I was no expert on hotels, but I did know a bit about slums, and this was one of the worst. However, we had no alternative, and after all it was only for the one night. The rooms were pretty shoddy with four single cots in each, with a kind of grey sheet as covering. An evening meal of sorts had been prepared, but one look was enough for me. It was some kind of rice concoction laced with rather pungent fish – I think? And as it had been a long, hot, and tiring day I decided to turn in. Our train for Cairo was leaving at nine the following day, and I think we were all feeling fed up not knowing what sort of ship we were headed for.

I soon dozed off, but at some time during the night I was awakened by a peculiar clicking noise. Curiosity got the better of me, so I pulled the cord that activated the light above my bed. To say I was taken aback would be an understatement. The bedroom floor was literally covered with the largest black beetles I'd ever seen. Of course my putting on the light woke my room mates up, and they were just as staggered as I was. For the rest of that night we sat up in our beds with the light on. This seemed to have scattered them back through cracks in the floor boards. The whole building must have been absolutely infested with them.

The moment that dawn broke we grabbed our belongings and got out of the Paris Hotel pretty quickly. Fortunately we managed to find a little coffee bar that was just opening, so stayed there until train time.

An interesting little episode that occurred at the Paris Hotel 'Doss-house', which doesn't sound humorous now, but at the time it occurred was hilarious, concerned the fact that the manager, who was a Greek, required us all to sign the hotel register. Eleven of our deck crew were from the Outer Hebrides and kept themselves very much to themselves, speaking only in Gaelic when talking to each other. This in itself puzzled our host, but as they signed the book one after another, he began to grow very indignant thinking he was being made a fool of. Everyone of the Hebrideans had the 'Mac' prefix to his name, and on the register one 'Mac' after another looked suspicious to say the least. We finally managed to convince him that the names were genuine – or maybe he just decided we were all barmy. In any case he accepted it.

We boarded the train at Port Taufiq which was to take us to Cairo, Egypt's capital city. I think the journey took about two hours. The reason I can't be exact about this is because I slept all the way due to our encounter with the Paris Hotel beetles.

We had a two hour wait at the main station in Cairo, but were ordered not to leave the precincts under any circumstances. I took my luggage and found a bench near to our departure platform, deciding to relax until train time. Unfortunately this wasn't to be, as I'd no sooner settled down to watch the colourful parade of people arriving and leaving Cairo, when I was suddenly surrounded by a crowd of Egyptians babbling at me in Arabic and waving a chocolate wrapper under my nose. I hadn't a clue what it was all about, and quite frankly I was starting to get worried. The situation seemed to be getting out of hand as one of the Egyptians had produced an ugly looking knife. When I attempted to get up and leave I was shoved back down onto the bench. Luckily, after about five minutes of this I was rescued by the Thomas Cook representative who was travelling with us. He had an Ascari with him, a sort of policeman, and my assailants quickly quietened down. Gradually the reason for their anger was explained. It seemed that some 'hero' had attacked a sweet vendor from behind, knocking him to his knees, and when he'd dropped his tray had stolen some of his goods and made off. The chocolate wrapper they'd waved under my nose had been found near the bench I was sitting on, so they thought I'd discarded it and that I was the thief.

They say that all's well that ends well, and to say the least I was pleased that it had all been sorted out, because at one point I thought I was going to have my ear sliced off. Out of sheer relief I gave the Egyptian vendor an Egyptian pound (a hundred piastres), and away they all went. As they disappeared I thought to myself, 'If I find the scum who stole that chocolate he'll pay me my pound back, and I'll have another pound's worth out of his nose.'

Our train was in by this time so off we went to get counted on board by the Thomas Cook rep, and I was glad to see the back of Cairo Station.

So at last we made it to Alexandria, and gathering our kit bags, soon arrived on the quayside. There anchored about half a mile off shore was the mystery ship we'd blindly signed on to away back in Glasgow. To my surprise it turned out to be the *Llandovery Castle*, another Union Castle ship, and an even bigger surprise was to find that it was now a hospital ship. We were to have some strange experiences aboard her, not all of them very welcome.

To be frank, I think that if we'd all had a choice at that moment, most of us would have chosen not to join a hospital ship. Somehow to me it seemed almost like a cop out. As if we were leaving the war behind to go sailing under the Red Cross Flag, protected from enemy action by mutual international conventions of respect for the wounded. To some, of course, this would seem

140

a good thing, but to myself, and certainly most of my Hebridean shipmates, it felt as if we'd been duped in Glasgow. But here we were, she needed a crew like any other ship, so we'd just have to get on with it. There'd be no point spending the next six months full of resentment.

We were ferried out to the *Llandovery Castle* and quickly settled in. She had a bo's'n and three bo's'n's mates, under whom the rest of us were divided into three watches of ten men each. The ship was in a pretty shambolic state, so the first week aboard was spent in washing down, painting and holystoning the decks until the worst of her neglect had been rectified.

After this, my watch was sent to rig the two cargo derricks over number one hold. These derricks are a type of lifting gear with which most merchant ships are fitted to hoist cargo aboard. The system used was to position one of the derricks over the ship's side and secure it in place with steel guy ropes. Another derrick would then be positioned over the hold into which the cargo was to be loaded, and the lifting cables of the two derricks joined together in what was known as a 'union'. With this set-up cargo could be lifted from the quayside by the outboard derrick and drawn inboard by the other one to be lowered into the hold. It sounds complicated, but with two experienced able seamen winch drivers operating them it's a very effective method of loading and unloading.

Once we'd rigged up the two derricks ready for use, the bo's'n came along to inspect our work. Later that day a barge was towed out to us and moored alongside, while we were all mustered on the forward well deck. This turned out to be an exercise to discover who were the most proficient winch drivers. On the barge was a block of concrete with a lifting ring embedded in it, and two by two we operated the winches and hoisted this aboard. We were apparently being judged by the smoothness with which we raised it, drew it aboard and landed it on the well deck.

Two of us were finally picked, myself and Lachlan McCrae, and we were then instructed to continue practising for the rest of the day. The bo's'n also told us that we'd be sailing the next day to pick up wounded servicemen, who after hospitalisation in Egypt were being sent home to Blighty. The trip would be under the control of the Red Cross, and was a humanitarian mission to exchange German and Italian prisoners with the same number of

British lads, who due to their appalling injuries were no longer fit for combat (and I must add, not for much else either).

On the following day a string of flat-topped barges carrying the German and Italian soldiers arrived alongside. It was only then that we realised why the bo's'n had made us practise winch driving so much.

Two at a time the stretcher cases were placed one on top of the other in a specially made long box with lifting eyes on each corner. Then under the expert guidance of our bo's'n we lifted them aboard where they were carried below decks to the wards. This carried on until the last of them was loaded. And if I hadn't been aware of the sheer rottenness and horror of war before, it was certainly brought home to me that day when I saw those lads. Legless, armless, blind and others with such terrible injuries that I cursed the politicians and megalomaniacs who had brought this situation about, whilst ensuring that they the instigators remained in little danger – except perhaps from too much rich food and drink. With that off my chest I'd better get off my soap box.

Now that our pitiful cargo was on board we wasted no time. It was up anchor, and north out of Alexandria harbour into the Mediterranean Sea. We were headed for Smyrna in Turkey, which if I'm not mistaken is now called Izmir. Shortly before we reached the Dodecanese Islands. We were joined by a Swedish Red Cross ship the *Drottningholm* which was engaged in the exchange of prisoners along with us – Sweden being a neutral country.

Together we sailed along the Turkish coast and towards nightfall anchored in one of the nicest harbours I'd ever seen. I was on the fo'c'sle head when we dropped anchor. Once the anchor gripped and we came to a full stop the water was so clear that I could see the anchor cable almost down to the sea bed even in fading light. I've often wondered if it's still as clear now in these days of pollution.

The following day we began the task of offloading the German and Italian lads onto barges moored alongside, which took all morning. The barges were then towed ashore to offload, and in the afternoon returned with our own British lads, when the whole heart-rending experience of loading began again. Some of these lads had been waiting months for repatriation, and in spite of the appalling injuries they seemed delighted to be back among their own people once more.

A particular memory that came back to me while I was thinking of that time was the kindness and tender treatment shown by the hospital ship's permanent medical staff towards all these unfortunate lads, whether they were enemy wounded or, as now, our own personnel. They were a credit to their regiment, the Royal Army Medical Corps (RAMC).

Finally, by the evening of our third day in Smyrna, we'd finished loading, so once more raised the anchor and set sail back to Alexandria, accompanied again by the Swedish *Drottningholm*. The two things that stand out in my mind about all these voyages were firstly the absolute lack of secrecy about our destinations compared to all the other ships I'd sailed in, and secondly the fact that we were sailing through the night lit up like Christmas trees. To those of us who since the war began had been used to a complete blackout at night it was a bit disconcerting. This was due to the Geneva Convention which stated that we had to be fully visible.

May the thirteenth was my twentieth birthday, and also the day we arrived back in Alexandria. My mate Lachlan and I were excused all night duties, and told to turn in early as we'd be called at daybreak to get our derricks ready to offload the wounded servicemen and start them off on their long journey home. Their war was over.

We worked all through the following day at our winches, and it was almost dark by the time the last barge carrying the wounded pulled away from our ship's side for the shore. We were all pretty weary by this time, so after securing the lifting gear were glad to go below for a meal and a good night's rest. Before we turned in though, the bo's'n and the CO (commanding officer) of the RAMC lads came to our mess-room and said we were to have two days off to spend ashore in Alexandria. The CO told us to enjoy our short break, because we were going to be busy for the next few weeks, and that our next trip would be to Tripoli.

After breakfast next day dozens of feluccas (small Arab sailing boats) were fluttering around our accommodation ladder, vying with one another for custom to ferry us to the shore so that we could sample the delights of Alexandria.

I teamed up with Lachlan McCrae and four other Hebrideans, and with a good breeze behind us we were soon skimming across

143

the harbour to be skilfully landed on the quayside to begin our short stay.

Under the guidance of the older sailors we made straight for the Rue De La Bourse, or as it was commonly called, 'Beer Street'. It was soon pretty obvious that it was simply a collection of clip joints, where as soon as you sat down a hostess would join you and attempt to induce you to, "Buy me one drink, Johnny." It appeared that to these girls every Tom, Dick or Harry was called Johnny, and if you were daft enough to buy them a drink they would be served coloured water for which you'd be charged an exorbitant price. So after a couple of beers we went off to explore the city.

Alexandria was in a celebratory mood, as the news had just come through that the North African Campaign was over, and a quarter of a million German and Italian troops were in captivity after throwing down their weapons in desperation. Rommel, their commander, had escaped.

That day we bumped into a lot of the Fifty-first Division, also known as the Highland Division, who'd played a major part in the Jerries defeat. Quite a few of them were gaelic speakers, so obviously my Hebridean shipmates quickly established common ground. While they pattered away in their native tongue I decided to break away and see what I could of Alexandria for myself.

Apart from the usual souvenirs that I bought for home, I found a little leather shop where you could pick out your own design and colours in leather and have them made up into a pouffe. I paid a deposit and was told to come back the next day for it. Of course, when I told my mates I had my leg pulled. They all jeered you've lost your deposit, sucker, and by the next day I was beginning to believe them. But I needn't have worried, because when I returned to the shop there was my pouffe all ready for collection. It was worth every piastre I'd paid for it, and it was certainly durable as my mother had it for over forty years. I like to think it gave her something to rest her feet on for such a long time.

I took my souvenirs back on board the ship and still had the rest of the afternoon free. So when one of the lads suggested packing up some food, hiring a felucca and having the felucca wallah take us for a trip around the harbour I jumped at the chance. It was a great run out and we had our food, picnic fashion, on the steps of the Ras El Tin Palace. This had been one of the Egyptian Royal Family's many homes, but since the old King Fouad had died the young King Farouk never bothered with it, and on that day it looked empty and neglected. Still, we enjoyed our trip and arrived back on board tired out, but contented.

The following day we certainly knew that our short break was over, as it was 'all hands on deck' to load the ship up again with supplies from lighters towed alongside. A great deal of the stuff was medical, so it looked as if we were off again as before. This time, however, there was no secrecy. As soon as we'd finished loading and taking on water and oil, an RAMC sergeant who was supervising the handling of the medical equipment, confirmed that we were heading for Tripoli to pick up more of our own wounded and bring them back to Alexandria.

We sailed at midnight, which meant that our arrival in Tripoli would be around dawn on the third day. It was approximately a thousand miles from Alexandria to Tripoli in Libya, and the old *Llandovery Castle* was never built for speed. When we finally arrived we found that Tripoli had a lovely dockside, and it was obvious that the Italians had had a major effect pre-war on its layout.

However, we had no time for taking in the scenery, because we'd no sooner tied up than ambulances and lorries began to arrive on the quayside with stretcher cases and walking wounded. This went on all day until we were loaded once more with these poor victims of war. Then without delay we cast off and headed back for Alexandria again.

The RAMC sergeant, who seemed to know what he was talking about, told us that transferring all these lads to hospitals in Egypt was to free up the facilities in and around Tripoli because something big was imminent – or at least being planned.

Over the next ten days we did two more round trips to Tripoli. And looking back, from the latter part of May 1943 and all through June we never seemed to relax at all. All shore leave had been cancelled at the Alexandria end of our runs, though we did manage a couple of hours ashore in Tripoli. However, apart from the fact that this gave us a chance to set foot on dry land there was nothing to see or do. The town was deserted and all normal commercial life didn't exist.

As far as I can remember we took our last shipload of wounded

g

back to Alexandria on or about the middle of June. We'd loaded up with supplies, fuel and water as usual and set off for Tripoli with another hospital ship, the Royal Fleet Auxiliary (RFA) *Maine*. The *Maine* had originally been named the SS *Panama*, and had belonged to the Pacific Steam Navigation Company, but was now attached to the Royal Navy exclusively and was their only remaining coal burning vessel. On this trip to Tripoli, however, we found the harbour was a hive of activity and our ship had a struggle to find an anchorage. It was obvious that something big was about to happen, though exactly what was a mystery. Even the RAMC sergeant, who usually had a good idea of what was going on, was in the dark. Though he promised to let us know as soon as he found out.

It was impossible not to notice the massive build up of ships and men all along the North African coast, but their exact purpose was obviously still a closely guarded secret. Being anchored in Tripoli harbour during the early part of June 1943 was, to coin a phrase, like 'waiting for the other shoe to drop'. Apart from the anchor watches and keeping the ship clean we were more or less left to our own devices. And then one day, completely out of the blue, we were told that shore leave had been granted and we were literally 'ordered' to go ashore. We hadn't a clue as to why, but there seemed to be air of urgency about. Anyway, boats were coming out at 1pm that same day to ferry us all ashore. And since we'd been given this order early in the morning I decided to fill in the time before departure by catching up on some letter writing; which as usual I'd been putting off. This wasn't plain procrastination on my part, but the difficulty I found in composing letters when we weren't allowed to tell our folks anything concerning our whereabouts or experiences. All I could say in a letter was simply that I was well and hoped they were too, and that I hoped to see them soon.

When I'd finished all my letter writing I decided to have a nap until the liberty boat arrived. This was fatal, for when I woke up the boat had been and gone and I'd missed it. There was another ferry due at four o'clock, so I decided to catch that and find out what I'd missed earlier on. When I finally got ashore I discovered that I was too late for everything. I'd apparently missed seeing King George VI, who'd flown in to see General Bernard Montgomery to congratulate him and the Eighth Army on their victory in North Africa, and to present him with his knighthood. Apparently Monty had given a speech afterwards from a hastily erected platform on the back of a lorry, exhorting those soldiers who were present to help him continue the fight 'over there'! At which point he'd pointed across the Mediterranean in the direction of Italy. My informant told me that at this most of his audience then expressed their preference not to follow him 'over there', and pointed westwards towards Blighty.

Whether this was true or not I don't know as I wasn't there, but my informant was usually spot on. Later that evening I spoke to quite a few of the 'Desert Rats', as they were affectionately known, and their feeling seemed to be that they'd earned a spell of home leave. However, they were doomed to disappointment, because as usual Tommy Atkins – the collective nickname for the poor old underpaid, ill-treated British Soldier – had no say in the matter.

I wasn't too let down by not seeing the King and Monty, but I was a bit miffed that neither of them had asked about me. However, I put this down to both of them having other things on their minds, so gave them the benefit of the doubt.

Wandering around Tripoli in order to prolong my trip ashore I found a little wine bar that some enterprising Libyan had set up. The problem was that I only had Egyptian currency which I thought would be unacceptable. But not a bit of it, these people were resourceful, and I think if I'd only had Japanese yen they'd have found a method of conversion. Anyway, I had a decent few drinks and caught the last ferry back aboard, not exactly blotto, but a long way from sober.

The following day it was 'up anchor', and we sailed to Benghazi to pick up some wounded. Then it was on to Tobruk to pick up some more, and finally on to Alexandria to land them. I assume that once they were fit enough to face the long journey they'd be shipped back to the UK and their families.

I think that everybody on board these hospital ships, from ordinary crew members to medical staff, were terribly affected by the sight of these casualties of war, whose wounds included every kind of injury from lost limbs to horrific burns and facial damage. The one overriding impression I retain is that a lot of them seemed to be utterly bereft of any will to go on. They looked totally dejected and bewildered. I dreaded to think what the future held for them. Most of them were little more than boys, who were going home to spend the rest of their lives in wheelchairs, or in a darkness of the worst kind, permanent.

The worst part of our job was that we were not seeing just one or two of these poor souls, but four or five hundred on trip after trip, and I personally never got used to it. Every ship load presented another tragic vision of man's inhumanity to man.

One of our bo's'n's mates was a huge Hebridean from South Uist in the Outer Hebrides. His name was Donald McCleod. Normally he was a rather taciturn individual, but on one occasion while loading some horrendous casualties I saw him standing by himself at the ship's side with his shoulders heaving and tears streaming down his face from sheer compassion. The sight of this giant of a man sobbing over these unknown heroes was one of the most moving experiences I've ever had. Fortunately he didn't realise that I'd seen him or I think he'd have been mortified, and of course I never mentioned it to him or to anyone else.

After three or four of these Benghazi/Tobruk/Alexandria trips, we were ordered back to Tripoli at the beginning of July and spent two days in Alexandria loading supplies. Once again the RAMC sergeant told me that something big was about to happen. He said they'd taken on board a lot of extra medical supplies, and his guess was that we were to follow, and lend support to an invasion somewhere. Once again his prediction proved to be uncannily accurate.

We arrived back in Tripoli I think about the 7th-9th of July 1943, and dropped anchor amid scenes of great activity among ships of every description. We'd no sooner hung our accommodation ladder over the side than our orders were delivered by launch. These were sealed and we'd have to wait to see what they were.

We lay at anchor in Tripoli harbour for two days before finally our orders to sail arrived. We raised anchor in convoy at almost dusk on the 10th of July 1943, and once clear of the coast altered course in a more or less westerly direction. This in itself was a mystery, and for once no one who knew was saying anything. By the numbers and types of ship in the convoy we were obviously part of an invasion, but where? Of course, everyone now thought of themselves as experts, and guesses ranged from Marseilles and various places on the south coast of France, to Corsica and

148

Sardinia. No one even thought of Sicily.

We'd soon passed Lampedusa Island, which unknown to us at that time had surrendered, and we were now sailing north-west between Cape Bon, Tunisia, and the Island of Pantelleria, which was under heavy air and sea bombardment but still doggedly resisting all attempts at capture.

As a hospital ship we were still lit up like a Christmas tree at night with our illuminated Red Crosses etc., so must have been visible for miles. After we cleared Cape Bon that night the weather took a turn for the worse. It was soon blowing a gale, turning the sea into a maelstrom. I think we all thought that this would put an end to any plans to invade 'anywhere', and as night wore on things got worse, blowing into a full force nine or ten gale.

At daybreak the next morning the seas were still heavy and breaking over the bow. I was on the 8am to 12am watch, and my normal lookout position would have been on the fo'c'sle head, but due to the bad weather I was sent up onto the wing of the bridge instead.

Just before nine o'clock the Skipper came up into the wheel-house and went into a huddle with the first officer. Then dead on the stroke of nine he gave the order, "Hard to starboard," and soon we were sailing in exactly the opposite direction to what we'd been steering all night. We were now heading for the Malta Channel which lies between Malta and the south coast of Sicily. I think it was then that the penny dropped, and the reason for our passage in the wrong direction became clear. It had been a decoy strategy, and with us being easily visible and sailing almost to Sardinia it would have given the impression that this was to be the invasion point.

Whether this was true or not it was the accepted theory aboard the *Llandovery Castle*, though no one would ever have admitted this, because to have used a hospital ship in this fashion would have contravened the Geneva Convention. Personally I could see no other reason for our sailing north-west for about fifteen hours, which at our speed must have been about two-hundred and fifty miles in the wrong direction . . . a very rum affair indeed!

On or about the 14th of July we arrived off Syracuse on the south-east of Sicily to the sounds of heavy fighting ashore. At that time we knew nothing of what was happening, and only learned later that the fighting was by British troops who had landed further south, and had fought their way to here under General Montgomery. The Americans, led by the notorious General Patton, were to fight their way up the west side of the Island; both armies to meet, hopefully, at Messina opposite to the 'toe' of Italy.

Of course, as I've said, we were unaware of all this at the time, or of the acrimony that existed between the two generals. It was, in fact, many years before this was all made public.

We entered the harbour with all our derricks topped ready for use, and judging from the noise of battle ashore we were going to be busy. We anchored about a mile from land and about a hundred yards from a sunken hospital ship called the *Talamba*. She belonged to the British India Steamship Company, and had been taking on wounded when she'd been attacked and sunk. She was sitting on the bottom perfectly upright, but with only her promenade deck above the water. The wounded men she'd been loading had been transferred to another hospital ship called the SS *Tairea*, and at that time we didn't know whether her casualties had been heavy or light.

Floating about the harbour were a number of bodies, though whether they'd come from the *Talamba* or not we didn't know. It seemed inhuman to leave them floating around like so much flotsam. At least our captain seemed to think so, because he ordered one of our lifeboats to be lowered to go and recover them. There were no such things as body-bags in those days, so we took linen sheets to wrap them in. It took us about two hours to recover the four bodies we could see. This was a gruesome business and we all felt glad when we were back on board – and even better when the captain sent for us and thanked us with a rather decent glass of rum. I never drank anything as welcome.

Of course the job with the bodies wasn't yet over, because before they could be given a decent burial at sea they had to be sewn up in canvas with a heavy 'fire-bar' at their feet to make sure they sank. Four of us were given this unenviable job under the guidance of the bo's'n who'd had experience of this task in the past.

We didn't waste any time, I can tell you, and where normal canvas sewing would have about eight stitches to the inch we made do with about one to the inch and soon got the job done. It would now be a matter of waiting until we were back at sea before they could be committed to the deep after a service held by the chief officer. At least it would be dignified.

However, we had no time to dwell on all this, because early the following day the wounded began to arrive from ashore and this kept us busy all day. When night came, instead of putting the derricks down in their housings we simply tightened all the guy wires. So although it was obvious that we were leaving Syracuse we knew we couldn't be going very far.

Early next day it was 'up anchor and on up the coast'. After about two hours sailing we arrived at a point somewhere between Augusta and Catania still on the eastern coast of Sicily. As we neared the coast we could once more hear the sounds of heavy fighting coming from somewhere towards Catania, and began cruising up and down at half speed while I think we were waiting for the signal to go in for casualties.

We entered Augusta late that evening and had no sooner anchored than they started arriving. There were quite a few stretcher cases and walking wounded who turned out to be a mixed bag of British, German and Italian troops. I've often wondered since if the people ashore who decided on who needed hospitalisation most had any system of priority by nationality, or was it simply by medical need. I like to think it was by medical need.

We finished loading under arc lights, and by midnight our wards were full and the operating theatres working non-stop treating the most severe cases. No time was wasted. We raised anchor and left for Alexandria with our cargo of suffering humanity. It seemed a great shame that the British lads who'd fought so gallantly across thousands of miles of African desert and came through unscathed, were now thrown into another campaign instead of being spared for their sacrifices and sent home. I suppose that the brass-hats had decided that because of their experience they were battle-hardened, and so would achieve a quicker victory, though I doubt if this would have been any consolation to the soldiers themselves.

At nine o'clock the following morning all normal activity on board was halted. Those of us who'd recovered the bodies from Syracuse harbour and subsequently sewed them up were assembled on the ship's after rails for the burial service. The ship's engines were almost stopped and the chief officer read a

151

simple service. Then one by one the canvas wrapped bodies were placed on a large board which rested one end on the rail, and committed to the sea. There was no pressure put on anyone to attend this ceremony, and yet the after deck was crowded with crew men paying their respects to four unknown servicemen who'd made the final sacrifice.

And so it was back to Alexandria, where on arrival we worked late into the night offloading the wounded. All of the deck crew were involved, and when the last of the casualties had been safely transferred ashore we set about securing all the derricks and preparing for sea again. Water, fuel and other supplies arrived the following day, and in company with another hospital ship, our old friend the RFA *Maine*, we set off for Sicily again.

We reached Sicily three days later and entered the harbour at Augusta, but the *Maine* left us bound for Syracuse. For us it was simply a matter of dropping the anchor which had hardly settled on the harbour bottom before the lighters of wounded began to arrive. On each trip now we were taking many more than the ship had been designed for, so I think casualties had been much heavier than was expected. One of the soldiers I spoke to was a Canadian, and he told me a story that at first was hard to believe. The American general, Patton, had allegedly stormed into a field hospital and dragged one wounded man out of bed, and threatened to shoot another one with the pearl handled revolver which he always carried in a holster like a cowboy. Apparently he didn't think their wounds were bad enough to exclude them from the battle. This seemed unbelievable at the time, but later the story was verified. They say that absolute power corrupts absolutely, and in this case it sounded true.

We did about three more of these round trips between Sicily and Alexandria during July and August 1943. But then on August 17th 1943 the island was finally captured when General Patton's army entered Messina a few hours before Monty with the British and Canadian lads.

We made our last trip at about that time and during our journey back to Alexandria we lost another three unfortunates who died of their wounds, and we, 'the undertakers' as some wit had nicknamed us, had to prepare them for burial at sea. As before this was a poignant occasion, but this time the obligatory snort of rum from the skipper was no consolation. I vowed that when we reached Alexandria I'd wash away the stench of hospitalisation with a good old booze up, and all my watch mates agreed.

So once again we landed our wounded in Alexandria, and when the ship was clear all the deck and engine-room crew were given three days off. All that was needed then was for the shipping agent to bring out our Egyptian currency – or for our skipper or chief officer to go ashore for it – and off we'd go.

This question of how merchant seamen were able to get local currency in foreign ports has cropped up before, so I'll try to explain how it works. Pre-war most shipping companies had agents in all the foreign ports they used. These agents would handle such things as: bills of lading, cargo manifests, etc., as well as arranging for fuel supplies, food and water and generally cutting through all the red tape on the shipping company's behalf. I came into contact with a few of them and as a rule found them very astute. To a skipper who invariably didn't speak the local language they were an absolute boon. As far as currency was concerned, a few days before we were due to dock in a foreign port a 'sub-list' would be circulated on which each seaman could request a certain sum of money for shore-going. Most skippers would usually halve this on the principle that the less we had to spend the less chance there was of us getting into trouble. And also, of course, because the less we 'subbed' the more we'd have at the end of the voyage. Once the ship arrived in port the skipper, or someone delegated by him, would total up the sub-list and the agent would bring this sum aboard in local currency.

This system didn't obtain in American ports, however, due to the currency restrictions in force at that time. Over there we'd be 'told' how much we were allowed, and I don't think that this ever exceeded about five dollars per man. So with the exchange rate at that time being around four dollars and eighty cents to the pound, we certainly weren't going to to able to go mad. Fortunately in both the USA and Canada the people were kindness personified, so the lack of cash when visiting those countries never stopped us from enjoying shore leave. To return to the agents again, there must have been a great deal of trust between them and their ship owner clients for I've no idea how they were repaid at that time. Maybe they simply had to wait until the war was over.

However, we eventually got our Egyptian piastres and went ashore by felucca to try and forget something of the last few weeks. I can't honestly say I enjoyed Egyptian beer, I think they brewed it with onions. And as far as the local rum, 'Bollanachi', was concerned it could have been used for engine fuel. Still, the more we drank the more bearable it became and our three days passed by in a haze.

After this short break it was back to everyday ship life and my old pal, the RAMC sergeant, came up with the rumour that we were on our way home and our spirits rose no end at this nugget of good news.

Apart from our normal duties some of the lads were 'seconded' to the the two ship's carpenters, who were busy building a wire enclosure on the starboard promenade deck. This consisted of strong wooden uprights and horizontal stiffeners covered by heavy wire netting. What it was to be used for we couldn't find out.

Towards the end of August we began to take on board quite a few stretcher cases, who we assumed must be going home to the UK to be reunited with families and friends, and to receive better medical treatment. For many of them it was all in vain. Nobody could restore the sight to a blind man, or limbs to those who'd lost them.

There were also victims of horrific burns who faced years of hospitalisation and painful skin grafts. We heard rumours going around at that time about a surgeon called Archibald McIndoe who was using new techniques on RAF pilots who'd suffered terrible facial burns. He'd apparently opened a hospital at East Grinstead, but at that time in 1943 we didn't know how successful he was, and wondered if he might be able to help some of these poor devils. We all certainly hoped so.

At last our chief officer confirmed that we were indeed going home, and would be sailing on the 23rd of August. And now that the Mediterranean Sea was relatively free of enemy action, that was to be our route.

Finally, the day before we sailed we took on board about fifty men suffering from shell shock. When I say 'men' I exaggerate. Some of them were only boys, and what a pitiful sight they were. Sadly, in those days, I don't think they were looked on very sympathetically by the powers that be. At best they were labelled inadequates, and at worst as cowards. I myself subscribed to none of these theories, and think that they were simply men whose resistance had been stretched to breaking point by experiences beyond there understanding.

The reason for the wire mesh cages now became obvious. These men would be allowed to sit in these cages during the day for fresh air, and the reason for the wire mesh was to prevent them from doing anything drastic. However, on the many occasions I saw them, on the long voyage home, I don't think they even knew where they were at all. They gave the impression that they were oblivious to reality. And when I thought that barring a miracle they were likely to be institutionalised for the rest of their lives I was filled with chagrin. These were the victims of war whom the people, on whose behalf they'd lost their sanity, would never see.

The night before we left Alexandria behind we were allowed shore leave until midnight. We took advantage of the break, but I'm afraid my heart wasn't in it. I spent a couple of hours buying cheap souvenirs etc., then caught a felucca back to the ship. I paid the felucca wallah off, and as I'd come to know him quite well I thanked him and gave him all my remaining piastres which I now had no further use for. To my astonishment when I got down to our living quarters I found all my mates had been of the same mind as myself and come back early. I think we had what came to be known as the 'Blighty Blues' and couldn't wait to be off.

At eight o'clock the following day it was 'anchor stations', and we left the Bay of Alexandria for what we hoped would be a long time.

I suppose, looking back over the years, it had not all been bad. The lads from the Hebrides had become good shipmates over the months. Donald McCleod, the bo's'n's mate, a very reticent bloke normally, paid me a compliment that I've always remembered. He said, "You're such a good seaman, that if you only had the 'Gaelic' you could be taken for a Hebridean." I thought, 'That's a backhanded compliment if ever I heard one,' but I knew what he meant.

Two little incidents particularly stand out in my memory of that voyage home. The first was a conversation I had one day with a young lieutenant. He'd lost an arm and an eye in the latter stages of the North African campaign. Apparently he'd done something very brave and had been cited for a medal. He thought he was destined for a desk job after recuperation. However, it was his remarks about his future that caught my attention and really made me see the rottenness of the class system that existed in Britain. He said, "I'll be glad when the war is over and we can get back to normality, afternoon tea at the Savoy and good old days at Henley with one's chums after the regatta." The astonishing thing to my mind at the time was his absolute conviction that this was 'normality' in Britain. He seemed blissfully unaware of the grinding poverty that ninety per cent of British people endured.

The second incident concerned a conversation I had with a Cardiff lad who worked in the engine-room. He told me of a talk he'd had with one of the wounded seaman we'd picked up in Syracuse earlier. This man was an Indian seaman who'd apparently settled in Cardiff, Tiger Bay area some years before the war. He'd been serving on board the hospital ship *Talamba* when it was sunk in Syracuse Harbour. He'd been wounded in the attack and had only just recovered enough to stand the journey home. The story he told our Cardiff engine-room lad was that the plane which had bombed and sunk the *Talamba* hadn't been a German aircraft at all, but he thought American. Whether this was true or not I don't know. What I do know is that at that period of the war the Yank pilots had probably caused more havoc amongst their allies than amongst the enemy. The words 'trigger happy' springs to mind.

So we were now on the final leg of our journey home. The only other incident of note was a prolonged scrutiny of us by a German aircraft shortly after we'd passed through the Straits of Gibraltar and out into the Atlantic. The aircraft stayed with us for almost ten minutes, and as it banked from port to starboard, flew near enough for us to see the pilot's face. What he was looking for I don't know, but he gave us a decidedly nervous ten minutes and a collective sigh of relief was heard when he finally waggled his wings and departed.

So there are my memories of my second invasion experience, which we later learned was called Operation Husky. My first invasion experience mentioned earlier, Madagascar, or at least my minute share in it, had not seemed as bloody as Sicily. I think in Sicily there'd been a disproportionate loss of life, and I've often thought that a better strategy would have been to blockade the island until they surrendered. That's probably why I'm not a general, I suppose, but at least it would have saved lives. The British and Canadians between them suffered almost thirteen thousand dead and wounded, and the Americans around ten thousand. All this in six or seven weeks from start to finish. I like to think there was another way.

In conclusion I should like to point out that all during this Sicilian campaign we, of course, knew nothing about the strategies involved. All that myself, and all the other lads involved whom I've spoken to knew, was that it was a hard slog against a determined enemy. Which was only too apparent from the numbers who fell.

18

Back in Blighty; and a Voyage to Nowhere

We arrived in Swansea, South Wales in the first week of September 1943, and after discharging our wounded were then given the choice of re-signing or not. I chose not, and on the 9th September I was paid off, feeling glad to see the back of the *Llandovery Castle*, and as I was due one day of leave for each month I'd spent at sea I was off home to Barrow for seven days to see my family and relax.

Looking back over the years, I think that those few days' leave I had in September 1943 were probably the most enjoyable I'd had since the war started. There were three other Barrow lads on leave at the same time, and as we'd all served on the same ships – although not together – we consequently had something in common. We'd meet during our morning visits to the shipping pool office to sign on – something we had to do once our allotted leave had expired. Mr Garland, who was still in charge of the office, would have details of all crew requirements nationwide, and being a wily old bird he wasn't averse to the odd trick to get crews.

In theory, although it was never put to the test as far as I know, a seaman could refuse the first two ships he was offered, but had to join the third. On arrival at Mr Garland's office to sign on, he would ask us quite seriously if we fancied joining a high-octane fuel tanker at say Falmouth which was sailing to the USA for a cargo. Naturally we'd say no, there were better methods of committing suicide. The following day he'd ask, still in his deadpan way, if we'd fancy joining an ammunition ship sailing to the Middle East. Of course these first two ships were fictitious, nevertheless our first two choices had gone and he'd then deliver his 'coup de grace' and offer us some stinking rust bucket of a tramp steamer that even a press gang couldn't have got a crew for.

Eventually, though, we got wise to him and whatever he offered first we'd accept, forcing him to admit his ploy. However, he wasn't a bad old chap and whenever one of 'his crew', as he called us, was lost he was as upset as if it was his own son.

After signing on each day I and the three lads on leave with me would usually spend the rest of the morning drinking coffee in Brucciani's Café in Dalton Road, trying to out-boast each other as to our exploits overseas. It was mostly harmless braggadocio and none of us believed anything the others said. At night we'd meet up again over a few pints and enjoy the crack again.

While I was on leave this time my older brother, Bill, was sent to Barrow to represent his regiment, the Grenadier Guards, and fire a volley over the grave of one of their comrades, a lad from Barrow-in-Furness. The cause of his death I never knew. This was the first time that Bill and I had met since the war began, and of course our mother was delighted, while we both really enjoyed the reunion after such a long gap.

At this time Jim, our younger brother, was somewhere out in the Atlantic with the Royal Navy on 'hunt and destroy' missions. He was sailing in HMS *Hurricane*, on which he was a leading torpedo operator. Obviously we didn't know this at the time and only found out later, in December of that year, when HMS *Hurricane* was torpedoed and sunk by a new type of acoustic torpedo which was apparently designed to be effective against the faster ships steaming between eight and twenty-five knots. It seems that the first torpedo strike had immobilised her propeller and rudder. But that wasn't enough for the U-boat, and without further ado they put another torpedo into an already helpless vessel. Fortunately, perhaps because they didn't have time, they didn't machine-gun the survivors as Grand Admiral Donitz had ordered them to do – undoubtedly with Hitler's approval.

Jim was picked up along with his shipmates and landed in Londonderry, Northern Ireland. How strange that three years before, after what had almost been a disaster in my first ship, SS *Fidelio*, I had been landed in Londonderry as well . . . coincidence

159

or fate?

They say all good things come to an end, and my short leave was soon over. One morning when I registered at the pool office Mr Garland had all my papers and my travel warrant ready for me to join a ship called the SS *Tamar* in Liverpool the following day.

For the first time in my life at sea I felt reluctant to leave after such an enjoyable ten days. However, orders were orders and off I went home to pack my kit-bag ready to join my new ship.

A little incident happened on that day that's as frozen in my memory as though it had happened yesterday. My mother had gone to the cemetery with a friend to put flowers on the friend's daughter's grave, so I decided to walk to meet them and break the news that I was off to Liverpool the next day. On my way I passed by the Blake Street Infant School, and through the open windows I could hear the children singing 'Now the Day is Over, Night is Drawing Nigh'. I couldn't help but stop and listen, and thought to myself that it didn't seem all that long ago that I was in that very school singing that same song at the end of a school day. It was a very touching sound and as I listened I thought of everything that had happened to me in the few intervening years. It was then I wished more than ever that the war was over, and that children like these all over the world could sleep peacefully in their beds at night, instead of waiting for the air-raid siren to send them scuttling like frightened animals into underground shelters.

Whether I actually thought these thoughts at the time I'm not sure, but I do know that the sound of those innocent little voices brought a lump to my throat.

The following day I said my good-byes and caught the train to Liverpool and the *Empire Tamar*. It was early evening by the time I boarded her, because my orders had said she was in Canada Dock whereas I found her in Brunswick Dock which was miles away.

As I climbed the gangway my heart sank. She was an old, pre-war tramp with crew's quarters forward in the fo'c'sle – deck crew on the starboard side, engine-room and stokehold men on the port. In fact a typical British slum of the seas.

I made my way into the accommodation which turned out to be one big space. Bunks in twos were built around the bulkheads and a stout, plain table for meals was in the middle. These would obviously have to be brought here from the galley amidships.

Some prospect in bad weather! As I entered there were eight or nine of my future shipmates sitting around the table, and it looked as if they'd just finished a meal. I glanced around and found an empty bunk which was right in the narrowest part of the cabin, and threw my kit-bag on it. Now I'd have to find the steward and get some bedding, also the bo's'n to let him know I'd arrived. Until this point none of the others had uttered a word, but then one of the younger lads at the table asked if I was the new AB. I said I was and he offered to take me amidships to the steward and bo's'n. The rest of them all muttered a few words, and I realised that they were all from North Wales – not noted for scintillating conversation at the best of times. Over the few years I'd been at sea I'd sailed with quite a few blokes from North Wales, and never met one who could be described as gregarious; and when it suited them they'd revert to talking in Welsh. I remember thinking, this was going to be some voyage. I'd only been aboard for half an hour, and I was sick of the ship already.

The lad who'd volunteered to find the bo's'n and steward for me was from Liverpool, so at least I'd have someone to talk to in a dialect closely resembling English, 'scouse', as opposed to listening to 'Gwigrich and Gogog', which is how Welsh sounded to me. The lad turned out to be a deck boy and this was his first trip to sea, so consequently he'd been appointed as 'Sailor's Peggy'. The origin of this term 'Peggy' goes back to the days of the old sailing ships, and the primitive surgery that was often necessary. If a sailor lost a leg he would be cared for on board until he was slowly able to get about again. The ship's carpenter would then make him a crude peg leg, which usually consisted of a leather cup for the stump to sit in attached to a round peg with a rubber ferrule on the end to prevent slipping. Obviously these sailors could no longer do the normal shipboard work, so were given cleaning duties, fetching food from the galley for the crew, etc. Consequently over the years any lad who did these very necessary jobs was nicknamed Peggy. Most newcomers to seagoing life have a turn at this, and I was no exception. According to the bo's'n on the *Llanstephan Castle*, however, I was a 'bloody awful Peggy'. Little did he know that I took this as a compliment. I hadn't gone to sea to end up as a skivvy, especially as I had two very adequate legs.

Anyway, the lad led me to the bo's'n's cabin, where we

knocked, entered and I was met by a chap of about forty. After I explained who I was he invited me into his cabin, which he shared with the ship's carpenter. This segregation from the deck and engine crews, who were as I've said housed 'forrad', was quite usual on old tramp ships. This was to prevent too much familiarity with the 'lower orders'. A typically British attitude.

The bo's'n then explained that he'd only been aboard two weeks himself, and as yet there'd been no official signing on, and also that he hadn't a clue as to what the ship's plans were. So in actual fact we weren't officially members of the ship's crew at all. And that until such time as we were all officially signed on the ship's articles we were free to come and go as we liked. The only officer aboard apparently was the captain, and he appeared to spend most of his time elsewhere, even sleeping ashore in a hotel.

I felt as though I'd joined a ghost ship, and what worried me most was whether we were going to be paid or not. I made up my mind that I would wait for the skipper to come aboard next day and get the situation clarified.

I went ashore that evening and spent the night at the sailors' hotel in Liverpool known as Gordon Smiths. Why it was called this I don't know, but it was probably named after some previous notable.

The following morning I returned aboard early to meet the skipper and find out what the programme was going to be, and while I waited for him I had a walk around the ship to acquaint myself with her. I don't think I'd seen a ship which had been allowed to get run down to such an extent as this one. She was filthy. She was a coal burner, and outside the doors to the stokehold were great heaps of ashes. The galley itself was dirty and neglected, and what the next ship's cook would make of it I couldn't imagine. There'd certainly have to be a 'helluva clean up' before it was hygienic again. The more I walked around the more disgusted I became. I wasn't looking forward to cleaning this lot up.

By this time the captain had arrived on board, and the bo's'n was rounding us all up to meet him. When we did we learned that he also was new to the ship. He simply told us all to book ourselves into the sailors' home until Monday, and then to be at the shipping office in Canning Place to sign on at ten o'clock. At this, one of the seamen from North Wales spoke up, I think on

162

behalf of us all, and told him we were all broke. This must have been anticipated, because we were then told to report to the steward's cabin where we drew a sub from wages we hadn't yet earned. And so retrieving my kit-bag from the fo'c'sle I went back to the sailors' home and booked in.

This was on a Friday night around the middle of October 1943, and one of the younger Welsh lads struck up a conversation asking me if I was going home for the weekend. When I told him it wasn't worth it he kindly invited me to spend Sunday in Birkenhead across the Mersey where his sister lived, having married a local man.

I accepted very gratefully, and spent a pleasant day with them. Within the bounds of stringent wartime rationing she produced a very nice Sunday lunch, followed later by a more than satisfying tea. Afterwards I thanked them for their kindness and caught the ferry back to Liverpool to await what tomorrow would bring.

On arriving at the shipping office on Monday morning the whole crew; firemen, deck crew etc., were assembled and we all duly signed on before making our way back to the ship. We were now, after almost a week of uncertainty, the official crew of the SS *Empire Tamar*.

The next day we began to clean up the ship and make her seaworthy. Fortunately over the weekend an army of cleaners had been working on board, and already had her resembling a ship once more. Within two or three days we'd taken on stores and water, so everything was really looking shipshape. All we had to do next was move to another dock where we took on coal. To my mind we hadn't taken on enough coal for a long voyage, so here was another mystery. No one seemed to know the answer, but finally two weeks after I'd first joined her we took the Mersey River pilot aboard and sailed.

We dropped the pilot at the Mersey bar and turned west towards the Irish Sea. At last we were on our way to somewhere, without an ounce of cargo and no idea of a destination, just hoping that all would be revealed in good time. However, our sense of well-being wasn't to last very long. I think we were about five miles off Point Lynas on the coast of Anglesey when the ship's engines suddenly stopped completely, and there we were at the mercy of the sea and weather. There was quite a heavy sea running, and being 'light ship' – having no cargo or ballast aboard – we were rolling about helplessly. Fortunately the wind was off the land, so there was no immediate danger of going aground. On deck we could do nothing but make sure the lifeboats were at the ready, though we hoped it wouldn't come to abandoning ship.

It turned out that one of the propeller shaft bearings had overheated, and nothing could be done until it cooled down in its own time. To have rushed in with artificial coolants could quite possibly have caused irreparable damage. I thought at the time that the captain had sent out a 'Mayday' signal, but if he had no one answered it. Night was approaching when to everyone's relief the ship's telegraph rang from the engine-room and the engines started up again. The tension had been palpable as none of us had relished the thought of wallowing about helplessly all night.

My watch ended at 8pm and as we were doing four hours on and eight off I was looking forward to a good sleep, hoping that tomorrow we'd find out where we were going. I must say that at the time I was too tired and fed up to worry about it.

All through that night we bucketed along at our top speed, which was a breathtaking eight knots an hour. I don't think that any convoy would have agreed to take the *Tamar*, as the speed of a convoy is naturally determined by the speed of the slowest vessel, and an eight knot convoy would have given Jerry a field day.

The following day my next watch, the 4am to 8am passed off without incident. We were now well south in the St George's Channel, and seemed to be heading for a port on the south coast. Which one, and why, were still unknown.

Everything seemed to be all right until about three-thirty that afternoon. I was sitting at the table in the fo'c'sle, having a drink of tea prior to my 4pm watch, when there was a massive bang which seemed to come from the bowels of the ship. At first we thought it was either a torpedo or a magnetic mine, and it was immediately all hands on deck. As I was coxswain of the starboard lifeboat I quickly made my way to the boat deck to take up stations. But as I passed the bridge the first mate called out, "Don't do anything yet. There's been an explosion in the engine-room, and we've sent out an SOS for assistance." It looked as though our time aboard was coming to an end, and candidly I thought 'the sooner the better'. Some ships just seem to be jinxed and this was one of them.

In about three hours a large tug appeared from the Bristol Channel and with good seamanship on the part of her skipper soon had a tow wire aboard us. Then began the long, slow drag to Cardiff Bay, where we were manoeuvred into an anchorage and safety.

For the next two days there was a constant stream of people visiting the ship – engineers etc. And then came the decision that suited me perfectly; we were being paid off. This was mainly, I suspect, because at almost forty years old the *Empire Tamar* was a write off. Another deciding factor must have been the steady arrival now of brand new Liberty and Fort boats that were being built in the USA and Canada.

I later learned that the *Tamar* was eventually loaded with ballast and deliberately sunk at Arromanches as part of the Mulberry Harbour created for Operation Overlord – the D-Day landings.

We were paid off on board and strangely, after I'd been given all my papers, money and documents, I was sent to the captain's saloon and asked a lot of questions by a very peculiar bloke. He wanted to know if I'd seen anything or anyone acting furtively since I'd joined the ship. Of course I made a joke out of it by saying that I'd sometimes seen the ship's cook acting in a peculiar manner as he mutilated good food. But from his expression I soon realised that this chap either had no sense of humour, or the matter was too serious for flippancy, so I promptly answered his questions sensibly.

That afternoon we were ferried ashore where I spent the night in the sailors' home before catching the train to Barrow the next day. On arrival I had to put up with a lot of good-natured banter all round due to the shortness of my trip. But because of the wartime secrecy situation I wasn't allowed to say anything, so just had to take it all in good part.

As I'd only been away for a few weeks I wasn't entitled to any leave at all, so the following day I went to sign on at the pool office, and to register the fact that I was available for another ship. After the signing on, Mr Garland told me he'd had a telephone call asking me to call in at the central police station at two o'clock, which in those days was in Cornwallis Street. I was as mystified as he was, and was on pins until I arrived at the station on time. Once there I was shown into an interview room to be confronted once again by a civilian. He asked me for a résumé of all I had seen and done since joining the *Tamar*. This didn't take long, but they seemed particularly interested in one of the firemen on board. I'd never even spoken to the man so could tell them nothing about him.

As this was my second questioning by what I assumed was the cloak and dagger people, it dawned on me that sabotage was suspected. Anyway, as I couldn't help them they thanked me and that was the last I heard of it. Personally I couldn't for the life of me see why anyone would want to sabotage an old rust bucket like the *Tamar*, but I suppose stranger things have happened. However, I was asked, no, more or less told, by the chap who interviewed me, not to say anything about it to anyone.

Of course, our town being Barrow-in-Furness the usual wartime expressions such as 'Walls Have Ears', and 'Careless Talk Costs Lives', didn't apply much, and when I arrived home for my tea I could see my mother was agitated. Apparently someone had spotted me either going in, or coming out of, the police station and had rushed to tell her. On the spur of the moment I told her I'd lost an identity card and I'd gone to report it. Whether she swallowed this or not I don't know, but she never mentioned it again.

19

Back on the Coastal Runs

Luckily I managed four of five days unofficial leave, but then around the middle of November I was sent to join another Empire boat in Barrow's Ramsden Docks. This was the *Empire Jack* which was at that moment being loaded with crates of war material.

The *Empire Jack* was an almost new coaster, and was in fact one of the two being built in Barrow at the time I joined the *Kyle Fisher* in 1942. I mentioned in that chapter how Captain Crowther had been disappointed at not being given captaincy of one of these new ships instead of the old *Kyle Fisher*. The *Empire Jack* was, in fact, owned by the Ministry of War Transport, but was being handled by Fisher's Shipping Company of Barrow. It was one of a type designed by the Vickers Armstrong's own drawing office at Barrow, and had hatch combing that almost reached the ship's sides. These wide hold openings enabled the ship to carry much wider loads than normal, such as complete gun mountings, even up to the sixteen inch heavy battleship armament built in Vickers' gunshop. These could then be delivered to wherever they were needed, which was obviously a much better system than having to bring the actual battleship all the way to Barrow to have them fitted.

I don't intend to dwell too much on my six months on the *Empire Jack*, as being a coaster it did not provide the kind of sailing I enjoyed, though it had its compensations. The *Empire Jack*'s skipper was a Captain Frank Poate who I came to have a great respect for, both as a ship's skipper and for his approach to his crew. Also for his seamanship – he was a born navigator. He came from the South of England, though exactly where I don't know. What I do know is that he made the six months I spent on the ship a pleasant time.

The mate (chief officer) was Billy Marshal, and as I'd signed on as ship's lamp-trimmer (bo's'n) we had to work hand in glove as regards cargo loading, and the hundred and one other things that make a ship run like clockwork. This was my first promotion from able seaman, and in retrospect I like to think I was up to the job. At least the skipper and mate seemed to think so.

Billy was from Appledore in North Devon, and I have happy memories of meeting his family when we made a trip there. He again was a man I grew to have great respect for, and during some hair raising experiences in our six months together I never saw him flap. His slow Devonian drawl was always reassuring. After the war he became a Trinity House pilot and I'm sure he made a good one. We met briefly once more in early 1970, when he was piloting a ship out of Heysham Docks, Lancashire. And although older he was still his old jovial self.

It was also during this six months period that we had more than enough hints that an invasion was being planned. We found ourselves carrying some peculiar machinery to ports on the south east coast, and saw at first hand the preparations going on for something massive. The manpower involved was enormous, and at every little inlet we entered there were camouflaged vessels. I'd like to make it clear, however, that although we saw this massive build up of men and materials ready for the greatest seaborne invasion ever contemplated, we had no idea at the time what it was all for. It was only later, after it had actually started, that we found out. The security clampdown had been a complete success.

Christmas-time 1943 we spent lying windbound in Sinclairs Bay, North East Scotland, and it wasn't much fun. Unbeknown to me it was during this time, on Christmas Eve, that my younger brother Jim was torpedoed, as I mentioned earlier. Thankfully he was rescued and landed without injury at Londonderry, but with only an old overcoat to his name. Our Royal Navy Sea Lords could be accused of a lot of things, but generosity was certainly not high on the list. At the time this happened Jim was only eighteen. Nowadays there'd be an uproar. They need counselling today if they miss the last bus home.

And so my six months on the *Empire Jack* came to an end. The skipper and mate both asked me to do another six months, but I refused. For although I'd only been at sea for four years my preferences were definitely still for deep sea ships.

As I've observed before, it's as well we can't see into the future, because six years later I was destined to rejoin the same ship. Though by then she'd been renamed the *River Fisher* and belonged to James Fisher & Son of Barrow. Talk about déjà vu, I even occupied the same cabin, and did the same job as six years earlier – though unfortunately not with the same crew.

h

20

A New Route to Old Ports

From time to time in these memoirs I've attempted to portray the mood of the people I came in contact with as the war went on. I think that until D-Day, 6th June 1944, the people of all age groups that I met and talked to seemed to have a sort of fatalistic attitude. We all seemed to think, 'this bloody lot is going on for ever'. But the D-Day invasion provided the catalyst for a wholly different feeling. Everyone I spoke to after that, particularly when the gallant Russians, despite great loss of life, turned the tide against Germany at Operation Barbarossa, now seemed to think that Jerry, although a long way from being beaten, was at last on the run. And as the allies gradually penetrated further into France the more the optimism grew.

As for my continuing part in all of this, after leaving the *Empire Jack* on the 12th June 1944, and spending four days at home on leave, I was sent to Gourock via Glasgow on June 16th to join the Royal Mail Company's ship RMS *Alcantara*. What a contrast to the *Jack*. As I approached her lying at anchor on the Clyde at Gourock I was immediately struck by her lines. She was all that I looked for in a ship; clean, sleek design and an overall look of efficiency. Later I learned that she was eighteen years old, about twenty-two thousand tons and had a speed of roughly twenty knots. I was both pleased and excited to be joining her, especially as each of her lifeboats looked almost as big as the ship I'd just left.

The *Alcantara* had quite a history. Built at Belfast in 1926 for the South American passenger and mail service, she'd been

170

converted into an armed merchant cruiser at the outbreak of the war. This was done to help out the Royal Navy, who were sorely stretched at the time, in their fight against German surface raiders. On one occasion the *Alcantara* had engaged in a sea battle against the *Thor*, Germany's most successful armed raider of that time. And even after she'd been severely hit herself she managed to close up on the raider, landing several of her own shells and forcing the raider to turn tail and run. But now she was back to carrying passengers in the form of troops to and from the various theatres of war, and I was proud to be a crew member of a ship with such an illustrious past. Looking back, I think I was then still very impressionable and probably naïve.

We left Gourock the following day and sailed to Liverpool. There, over the next week, we picked up cargo and a full complement of troops, then set sail once more for parts unknown. We'd formed a small convoy with a ship called the *Keranja*, also the Polish ship *Batory* – which I'd been in convoy with before – and another ship belonging to the Furness Withy Shipping Company. I think her name was the *Dominion . . ?* something or other, but I can't really remember. As escort we had two of the newer fast frigates that had now come into service.

We must have been an impressive sight as we steamed at twenty knots through the St George's Channel and out into the Western Ocean. This was to be a new experience for me, and I dare say for most of the other crew, for although our course had taken us well out from the Bay of Biscay to avoid any lurking U-boats, we eventually turned east and entered the Mediterranean Sea through the Strait of Gibraltar. This was now possible because the allies had finally made the 'Med' enemy free. The result being that it saved us having to make the seven thousand miles extra journey round the Cape of Good Hope to reach the Middle East or India. This fact in itself was enough to reinforce our belief that at long last an end was in sight.

At that time, of course, we knew nothing of the unspeakable horrors perpetrated by the Germans and Japanese on both civilians and service personnel. In my humble opinion both of these nations should have been classed as pariahs and treated accordingly after the war, and not allowed to grow and dominate the world economically as they eventually did.

Our convoy carried on through the Mediterranean until we

171

reached Port Said (Port Welcome). There we embarked some local boatmen together with their boats and a searchlight, all of which were needed for our journey through the Suez Canal. The searchlight was for night-time navigation, and the boats were in case we had to stop for any reason and tie up in one of the canal's lay-byes. In that event our derricks would hoist the men and their boats over the side to take our mooring ropes ashore.

An ever present danger in the canal, apart from ships travelling in the opposite direction, were sand storms. When these blew up it was impossible for ships to travel on, so they had to stop and be tied up. I was only caught in a sand storm once on the canal. We had to tie up, and when it was over the amount of sand on our decks was unbelievable.

I would like to emphasise at this point the absolute blessing that the Suez Canal was for all shipping going to the Near and Far East. It must have paid the cost of its excavation thousands of times over and was a credit to the French engineer Ferdinand de Lesseps who was responsible for its construction. A monument to him stands (or did then) on the Mediterranean end of the Canal at Port Said. Unfortunately De Lesseps' attempt to emulate this success at Panama was a failure. Though I think this was because he was unable to get proper financial backing.

I was to sail through the Suez Canal on several occasions as time went on, and whenever I did, something I was taught at school from the Bible used to cross my mind: 'Why on earth would Moses need to part the Red Sea so that the Jews could reach their so called 'promised land', when until the canal was dug they could have walked to Egypt and kept their feet dry?' Still, I suppose this wouldn't have sounded as dramatic as the old myth, and Charlton Heston would also have been denied his Oscar.

Once we were through the canal, it was down the Red Sea, past the impressive rock formation known as The Twelve Apostles at its eastern end, through the Strait of Bab el Mandeb, which is the waterway between the Horn of Africa and the Arabian Peninsula, then out into the Indian Ocean and on to our destination, Bombay.

We spent a week there disembarking troops and offloading cargo, before the process went into reverse and we loaded other cargo and troops for the homeward run and left India behind again. This time we had over a thousand Indian troops, Sikhs,

172

etc., on board plus a regiment of Gurkhas, all destined for the European campaign.

We passed back through the Suez Canal once more into the Mediterranean, and anchored at Port Said. Here I had the chance to renew acquaintance with Jock McGregor, an Egyptian trader who sold almost everything, and would take anything in exchange; cigarettes, clothing as well as any type of currency. I dealt with him often and he never once twisted me. Though having said that he always came out the better in any bargaining.

After leaving Port Said we passed through the Straits of Messina, between Sicily and the toe of Italy, to Naples where we disembarked our Indian friends and some supplies.

Naples Harbour was in a hell of a mess and we had to moor to a sunken ship over which a makeshift gangway had been constructed. Either our bombing had caused this devastation, or Jerry had dynamited things to deny their use to the allies, I'm not sure which.

We were allowed ashore and a crowd of us went off to visit the famous Galleria, a closed area of shops and restaurants which was very impressive. One particular alleyway led to the famous San Carlo Opera House, though unfortunately it was closed. But at least I could say that I'd stood outside it, as I had at the Metropolitan Opera House in New York. So I suppose I could claim to have walked in the footsteps of the great singers.

We left Naples after taking quite a few wounded, but mobile, soldiers on board. In spite of their wounds they were all pretty glad to be Blighty bound. From then on it was full speed ahead for home, and on the 17th August 1944 we docked at Canada Dock in Liverpool.

After disembarking the troops, Liverpool stevedores arrived on board to offload the cargo and we crew were all discharged. When we signed off we were asked if we'd like to sign on again for another voyage. I immediately said yes, for the simple reason that I liked the ship and had made some good mates during the last voyage.

As I was leaving the signing off room the bo's'n was waiting for me with one of his bo's'n's mates. He asked me if I was signing on for another trip, and when I replied yes he said how would you feel if I promoted you to bo's'n's mate next trip. Naturally I said I'd be delighted. "Right then," he said, "go with

Bill here and he'll show you the ropes." He then pointed out the one drawback. "You'll have to come to terms with the fact that from now on you'll be in charge of men, and not one of them," he said. This made me pause a moment, but I'm afraid that ambition won in the end and I took the offer. I suppose that at twenty-one, to be a bo's'n's mate on a huge liner was too heady a prospect to resist, and again it was an ego booster to be thought good enough to do the job. So the following day I signed on.

Since my very first arrival in Liverpool and my trip on the *Alcantara* events had moved very quickly. I was now a bo's'n's mate, and frankly it was taking some getting used to. I was beginning to realise, unfortunately, that being in a position of authority and having to make spur of the moment decisions was alien to all that I believed in. One of the other mates, who'd been seconded to show me the ropes, was a decent sort of chap who from time to time gave me good advice which on quite a few occasions brought me down to earth with a bump.

Before I go on, however, I'd like to insert something here that had happened on our previous trip, but which had completely slipped my mind. The day before we'd sailed from Liverpool on that trip, a party of about forty civilians, all foreigners, had come aboard and one of our crew members who was a Greek, George Boussateli, told us they were something to do with the Greek Royal Family. At that time the Greek monarch was George of the Hellenes, to give him his title, and through marriage etc., was related to most of the royal families in Europe. Our Prince Philip was one of them. At the outbreak of war I think they'd decamped to the UK. But now that the end of the war was in sight they were expecting to make a triumphant return to a grateful nation. Well, if that was their reasoning they came unstuck.

About fifteen of the Greek party turned out to be a marching band, and during the voyage they used to rehearse on the after deck on most days. It seemed that they were to lead the parade of returning dignitaries from the harbour at Piraeus to the capital, Athens. As far as bands were concerned they left a lot to be desired, in fact they were hopeless, being out of tune most of the time.

When we sailed into Piraeus Harbour and dropped anchor we could hear the sound of sporadic gunfire from ashore. There was apparently a virtual civil war going on between two different

174

factions, the 'Eras' and the 'Elan'. Who they represented I don't know, but they were obviously united in one respect; they didn't want our party to land. It was therefore decided that they should be taken on to Port Said for their own safety.

Meanwhile, one of the boats that came out to us selling trinkets had a relative of our Greek lad George Boussateli on board. And George, deciding that he'd be more use to his family ashore than here, asked our watch to cover for him while he made good his escape. We did better than that, we all pooled our resources; meagre though they were, and made him a decent bundle of chocolate, cigarettes and anything else we could find for him to take with him. As soon as it was dark we lowered a rope ladder over the side to his waiting boat. Then after wishing him well said good-bye. I thought at the time that if I ever went back to Greece in the future I'd make enquires as to how he'd fared. Unfortunately, however, I've never been to Greece since then.

Now it's back to my second voyage on the *Alcantara*. For the two weeks before we sailed, and until all the deck crew, engine-room crew and catering staff joined the ship, the bo's'n had me familiarising myself with every aspect of the ship. I spent my days climbing masts, checking rigging wires, shackles etc., and where necessary making lists of everything that needed renewing. This was all prior to the arrival of the deck crew, who would eventually do all these jobs under the supervision of the bo's'n and we three mates. It seemed strange that instead of being told what to do I would now be doing the telling.

My mentor, Bill Jones, who was one of the other bo's'n's mates, told me to always try and realise the potential of the lads in your watch. And never to humiliate any of them in front of their shipmates. If you do, he warned, you'll create a feeling of resentment among them all, and every job you ask them to do will be done reluctantly. These were wise words and stood me in good stead during the next six months.

At last all the crew arrived and we started to embark our passengers. These were mostly soldiers, but with quite a few Royal Navy lads; well over a thousand altogether complete with all their equipment. There were also a hundred or so men and women of the Field Auxiliary Nursing Yeomanry, commonly known as 'Fanny's'. Since the war ended I've heard one or two different names put to the initials FANY, but I prefer the one I've used here, because that's the name one of them told me they stood for.

This group were going out to Meerut in India, which was where the army had its pay corps headquarters as well as other administrative sections. They were a thoroughly nice crowd and I made quite a few good pals among them. I soon noticed that their catering arrangements were a kind of hit and miss stampede, and was able to help them out with a parcel of decent sandwiches now and then; for which the whole bunch of lads and lasses were very appreciative.

After they'd left the ship in Bombay and travelled north to Meerut I had a few 'thank you' cards from them, and they all said that the occasions I could smuggle them a little extra food were highlights of their voyage.

I've often said, and I'm sure most servicemen would agree, that our troops were sent overseas in conditions that if they'd been cattle would have had the RSPCA shouting cruelty. One of my earlier ships had once carried a regiment of Australian soldiers to the Middle East, and I've never seen such egalitarian treatment. The officers saw to all their men's problems, and tried their utmost to make shipboard life bearable. And yet the Aussies showed just as much, if not more, respect towards their officers as the British troops did. This of course was the British class system again at its worst.

In mid-September 1944 there'd been some desperate late attacks by the odd U-boat, and whether this was the reason or not, when we left Liverpool we once again joined a convoy. Luckily they were all twenty-knotters so we weren't going to be sitting ducks. However, for some reason, instead of going through the Mediterranean we headed south for the Cape of Good Hope and the long way round. There was some speculation at the time that we were to pick up some VIPs in South Africa, but if we did I never saw them. We by-passed Cape Town and sailed on to Durban, where we spent a few days before sailing on to India, Bombay again.

Bombay was becoming a second home to me. Even the gharri drivers greeted me like an old friend. A gharri was a horse-drawn carriage similar, I think, to our old hansom cabs although with a covering only used in bad weather such as they got in the monsoon season.

Our troops disembarked and we said cheerio to our friends from the FANYs. We stayed in Bombay for about a week before sailing south and east around the tip of India between it and Ceylon, then on up the coast to Calcutta where we anchored in the Hooghly River. This was an operation in itself because the ebb and flow of this river was so great, and the tide so strong, that we couldn't actually use the anchor in the normal way at all. We had to unshackle it from its chain and then manoeuvre the ship alongside a huge buoy and shackle the anchor chain to that. It was quite a long job, but according to the river pilot absolutely necessary.

As regards these pilots of the Hooghly River, they were apparently the creme de la creme of Trinity House Pilots. The river they worked on was so treacherous with its strong currents, that only the very best were allowed to pilot it. When they boarded a ship to take it up or down the river they had a small entourage of Indian servants with them, and were treated like potentates. The pilots were without exception British, and I've heard it said that in pre-war days their children used to be sent home to England to attend top rank public schools. This was in the days of the Raj.

However, a story that tickled me, and I know it's true, was about an old, rust-streaked tramp steamer that arrived at the mouth of the river and signalled for a pilot. When the pilot's boat came alongside the pilot saw that the ship had only put a rope ladder over the side for him to board. This wasn't good enough for the dignity of the pilot, so he shouted up to the skipper on the ship's bridge through a loudhailer that he required the accommodation ladder – which was a much more elaborate affair – to be lowered for him. A voice from the bridge shouted back, "No! You come up the rope ladder." The pilot, by now indignant at this treatment; shouted back, "Do you realise I'm the Hooghly pilot?" The old skipper, not to be moved, shouted back, "I don't care if you're Pontius Pilot, you'll come up the rope ladder." And eventually the pilot, realising he'd come up against a stronger character than himself, had to climb up the ladder alone leaving all his entourage on the pilot cutter.

My witness to all this said that neither of them spoke to each other all the way up river, but when they reached the limit of the pilot's jurisdiction the old skipper said, "Many thanks," and held out his hand. The pilot hesitated a moment then took the the other's hand. They both grinned and the acrimony was forgotten between the two stubborn old seamen.

Our cargo was soon discharged, and then began the job of letting go from the buoy, reconnecting the anchor to the chain and heading off back down the river.

Once we were clear of the Hooghly River we turned east across the Bay of Bengal, and eventually arrived at a point about halfway between Chittagong and Cox's Bazar on the coast of Burma where we dropped anchor in a deep water anchorage.

Nothing happened on the first two days and speculation was rife as to what was going on. During this time, however, the bo's'n told me to take my watch of twelve men onto the promenade deck and holystone the port side decks, while my opposite number, Bill Jones, had his watch doing the same thing on the starboard side. I thought this a bit incongruous at the time, but I think the bo's'n's idea was to use this opportunity to get some cleaning done while there were no troops on board. Holystoning is a practice that is carried out on all passenger ships, and though it's a tedious job I must admit that the decks look well afterwards. What it involves is wetting the wooden deck and sprinkling it with sand, then dragging the holystones to and fro over it to 'sand scrub' the surface of the deck. These holystones are oblong lumps of limestone, approximately a foot long, which are each held in a steel bracket with a long handle. After an hour or so of this treatment the sand is hosed away and the effect is very pleasing to the eye.

Apparently the name holystones originated in the days when the old wooden-wall, man-o'-wars of the British Navy used to anchor in the Solent off the Isle of Wight to take on provisions – the island being the great supplier of beef, wheat, milk, beer, etc., to the Royal Navy in those days. My cousin, Alan, who lives on the island tells me that the original 'holystones' came from the ruins of the old church at St Helens on the island which stands on the edge of the Solent. Most of the church had over the centuries gradually collapsed onto the beach leaving only the tower standing. The ship's crews apparently discovered that the stones from the church were ideal for scrubbing the decks, so they used to gather them off the beach, hence the name 'Holy Stones'. The church tower still survives to this day, having its seaward side

178

reinforced and painted white as a 'Sea Mark' . . . another little nugget of information I've learned.

To return to our own holystoning off the coast of Burma, there's one little incident I recall from that time which shows that whatever the situation there's always someone who can beat the system, or at least 'try to', whatever it is. I noticed that during the deck stoning one of my squad was pulling his holystone to and fro quite effortlessly with one hand. On closer inspection I saw that he was leaving three little furrows in the wet sand behind the stone. This obviously required discreet investigation, so I waited until 'smoko' time (brew up time) when the lads went off to their mess for a smoke and a drink. Then I lifted this clever character's holystone and found that he'd positioned three crown corks from beer bottles underneath which acted as good as castors. I threw the crown corks over the side and never said a word when the lads returned. However, the look on the guilty lad's face was enough to show he knew he'd been rumbled, and from then on he was a changed man. At least he tried no more scams.

While we'd been busy trivialising over clean decks, we later learned that there'd been two Japanese submarines on the prowl in the Bay of Bengal. It seemed they'd become separated from their supply ship, which had probably been sunk, and they were undoubtedly determined to do as much damage as they could.

On our third day at anchor we were approached from the north by a destroyer and a smaller mine-sweeper-type of vessel. On their decks they were carrying about two-hundred British soldiers, and it was plain that our skipper knew what was going on because he displayed no element of surprise.

The two ships tied up alongside and without delay we lowered our accommodation ladders port and starboard, and somewhat wearily our new passengers began to board. For the most part these lads looked gaunt and war-weary. They turned out to be from Orde Wingate's famous and feared Chindits, who'd operated in groups deep in the Burmese jungle behind Japanese lines. Orde Wingate, along with others, had proved that this kind of long range penetration could be very effective. But sadly Wingate himself was killed in an air crash and never saw the end of the war, or the results of his unorthodox theories.

Most of these men were thin to the point of emaciation, and were suffering the effects of constant bouts of malaria and other

179

tropical ailments. Fortunately for them our captain was a very kindly and understanding man. He called the chief steward up to the bridge and told him in no uncertain manner that they had to be fed on the best that the galleys could produce, and whenever they wanted it. This was the talk of the ship for days, though I don't think anyone begrudged them their special treatment – they'd gone through the mill enough.

Once all the troops were aboard it was 'up anchor', and with the destroyer and mine-sweeper as escorts to port and starboard we set sail back to Bombay.

We sailed through the Palk Strait between the southern tip of India and Ceylon, then finally north again to Bombay. This time we began loading almost as soon as we'd tied up, taking on board a regiment of Indian troops plus quite a few returning civilians. Who or what they were I don't know because they seemed quite a reclusive crowd, though they were obviously some higher echelon of Indian Civil Servants.

During that trip north to Bombay a tragic death had occurred. One of our Chindit soldiers had been found dead in his bunk, and it was thought that he'd succumbed to the illnesses he'd suffered from. Under the circumstances it was quite impossible to hold any kind of post-mortem, so he was buried at sea the next morning. Fortunately, on the *Alcantara* we carried a proper 'sail-maker' who attended to anything to do with canvas, so the job of sewing up the body fell to him. Which was a relief because I'd already had that dubious honour on the hospital ship and never wanted to have to do it again. The sail-maker told me later that the poor Chindit was so emaciated that he'd had to sew extra weights in to make sure he sank. Fortunately also, there was an Army Chaplain aboard, plus all his comrades, so at least they gave him a decent farewell. A sad end to another young life that had never really been lived.

Fully loaded with cargo and troops we left Bombay just before Christmas 1944, and would celebrate it, if that's the correct word, on the way to the Middle East. Of course it meant nothing to most of our passengers who weren't Christians. So apart from the Chindits, who thoroughly enjoyed it after all their deprivation, it was a pretty subdued affair for the rest of us. However, at least our normal 'board of trade' cuisine improved on Christmas Day. Also the bo's'n and we three mates were invited to the chief officer's quarters on Christmas Day evening. Which was quite enjoyable except for the fact that I and my watch were on lookout duty from midnight, so drinks were obviously limited.

On our journey up the Red Sea it was warm during the day but 'overcoat cold' at night.

Fortunately we saw no enemy activity on that trip, although lookouts were increased in case one or more of the Jap subs were roving about still trying to justify their existence. The chief officer told us that these were the most menacing type. They'd almost certainly know by now that the war was lost as far as they were concerned. Their supply ships were all sunk, but being so fanatical there's no way they would surrender, and like cornered rats would be at their most dangerous. Luckily we saw nothing of them.

We didn't stop at Port Taufiq, but carried on through the Suez Canal to Port Said and tied up. Here we disembarked our Indian troops before sailing on to Alexandria to pick up more. The first aboard were almost a thousand German prisoners of war, all ex-Rommel's Afrika Korps. They'd probably been held in camps somewhere in North Africa until transport became available. None of them were very old and frankly were quite docile. I think they'd long realised their war had been lost and were trying to make the most of the situation until repatriation. One of our officers had been told that they were on their way to Italy to start work on some sort of reconstruction of war damage.

The Germans were in the care of about fifty British soldiers and NCOs, and it didn't take long for them to embark. The British guards kept shouting words like 'Raus!' and 'Schnell!', but the Germans didn't seem to be taking a blind bit of notice. I only learned later what these words meant, but at the time the extent of any German I knew had been gleaned from such comics as the *Wizard* and the *Rover*. Also as a lad my favourite author was Herbert Strang, who'd interlaced his stories with, 'Schweinhund!', 'Got in Himmel!' and 'Donner und Blitzen!'

One of the sailors on my watch was Danish, and it was an eye-opener for me to listen to him speaking fluent German to some of the POWs. I realised then how limited an elementary school education was, and without sounding conspiratorial I think the policy was deliberate. In my day the 'chosen' were picked and received special treatment, being sent to either grammar schools or technical colleges, while the rest of us, invariably coming from the poorer homes, were to all intents and purposes abandoned and condemned to a life of menial and ill-paid jobs. I determined that day to try and learn some other language apart from my own, if only to find out what the different nations thought.

Another incident that tickled me at the time occurred while I was bartering with the POWs for military memorabilia. I'd exchanged some cigarettes for a leather belt from one of them, when I noticed that the buckle had the inscription 'Gott Mit Uns' (God With Us). I thought this most peculiar as 'we'd' been told ad nauseam that he was with 'us' and that the Germans were on the Devil's side. I've often pondered since on such a fickle deity who dispersed his blessings so willy-nillingly.

We were supposed to sail from Port Said on a Monday, but were held up at the last minute to wait for more passengers. It appeared that these were two hundred troops who'd been expected to cross over the bridge at El Kantara but had been delayed. They arrived next morning in a convoy of trucks, and as they alighted I'd never seen such a rag, tag and bobtail crowd in all my life. It turned out that they were a battalion of Jewish soldiers who for one reason or another had joined the British Army. They had all been members of the 'Haganah' or 'Palmach', who from what we'd heard from soldiers who'd served in Palestine, were groups adamantly opposed to a British presence there at all. So why they'd chosen to help the British was a mystery. Especially as two other organisations, the Stern Gang and the Irgun Zvai Leumi, who were also violently opposed to the British mandate in Palestine, were planting bombs and killing British soldiers regularly.

Isaac Stern, who'd formed the Stern gang, was later killed. The Irgun on the other hand survived and had among its members two future prime ministers of the State of Israel, Menachem Begin and Yitsak Shamir. These people were all followers, or believers in, the doctrines of Jabotinski, a Polish Jew who fervently believed that all Palestine was their promised land, and that eventually they would drive out the Palestinians and occupy it all . . . I note sixty-five years later that they've almost done it, by hook or by crook.

Apparently they pinned their expectations on what had become known as the Balfour Declaration (made in 1917 when Britain had been given a mandate for the area following Turkey's defeat in the First World War). This in truth was not a declaration at all, but simply a letter of intent that the British Government would assist the Zionist movement to attempt to establish a 'homeland for Jews' in parts of what was then known as the Levant and Trans Jordan. This declaration, however, also stipulated that 'nothing shall be done which may prejudice the civil or religious rights of existing non-Jewish communities in Palestine.' By what authority Lord Balfour had given these assurances is still a matter of some debate.

Of course the end of the war would bring horrific evidence of Nazi atrocities in Europe against not only people of the Jewish faith, but also against Gypsies, Slavonic peoples, or in fact, anyone whom the German Hierarchy classed as 'Unter Mench', or sub-human. However, more of that later.

As we helped these lads aboard with their equipment, I decided to find out as soon as I could their reasons for joining the allied war effort at this late stage in the fighting.

For the voyage to Italy the Jewish troops were given a section of the forward decks to meet and get the benefit of fresh air. The German POWs were kept well away from them for obvious reasons. During the short trip to Taranto I had to liaise daily with the captain of the Jewish battalion about various matters, such as having their equipment, etc., ready for disembarkation because they were to be the first ashore. During these contacts I made it my business to help them as much as possible because they seemed completely lost; and certainly no one from the British Army did anything to help them integrate as far as I could see. In the course of these meetings I had quite a few serious talks with the captain and some of the other officers and men. One remark I remember from the captain struck me as odd. He said, "The end of your war is in sight, but ours will then begin." When I asked him to clarify this statement he replied that Palestine was theirs by right of history, and that once they'd driven the British out they would set about removing the indigenous people, so that once and for all they'd have a homeland of their own. Free from the fear of pogroms and anti-semitism.

While I agreed with him in principle I pointed out that the Palestinians (also a Semitic race) might raise objections, but this was brushed aside as of no importance. What he was saying, and this was almost sixty years ago, was that there was a new feeling of 'can do militancy' among these Ashkenazim Jews of a younger generation. While I admired their gusto I remarked that it was a risky strategy, and tried to point out that Sephardic Jews had lived peacefully alongside their Arab neighbours for hundreds of years, but the captain just laughed at me indulgently. However, what I'd really been trying to find out came from one of his young lieutenants. He told me that they'd joined the British 'under instruction'. Firstly to ingratiate themselves with the mandate authorities, who were the British Government, but principally to learn the day to day techniques and paraphernalia of soldiering which they could use at some future date.

I hope that anyone who is au fait with the situation in the Middle East, then and now, doesn't think I'm trying to sound as if I knew then what would happen in the future. I'm simply relating my memories of those conversations, and the deeply held belief of those young men. What I objected to was the main thrust of their reasoning, which was that they had the right to displace a whole nation in order to create one for themselves. I told them that a lot of bloodshed and anguish lay ahead of them if they did this. Sadly, I have been proven right.

My daily patrols around the ship involved such things as checking all the lifeboats on each side of the boat deck to make sure they were ready for instant use, as well as keeping an eye on how my twelve watch members were getting on with whatever jobs they were on. During the course of these rounds I could see that intensive bargaining had obviously been going on between our crew members and the German POWs. Most of our crew now seemed to have Afrika Corps caps on – I think this could have been the beginning of the baseball cap craze – and though no cigarettes had been issued to the Jerries most of them were smoking and minus most of their gear.

One night, as I was doing my rounds on the promenade deck, there were about a hundred Germans sitting in the shadows with an accordion playing *Watch on the Rhine*. I couldn't understand the words they were singing, but it was touching to think that it would be some time before they saw their beloved River Rhine again. The following day I asked our German-speaking Danish lad what it was that so enthused the Germans about the Rhine. He explained that this dated away back into their history. To the

184

Germans the River Rhine had always stood between them and their enemies, and thus the fate of the Rhine was their fate too.

We landed at Taranto in Italy where most of our troops were to disembark, and the Jewish lads were the first off. Their captain, with whom I'd had such lively discussions came to say good-bye. He thanked me for all the help I'd given them, and we wished each other well for the future. Frankly I feared for his future more than for my own.

At first I'd wondered why they were chosen to be first ashore, but then I found out that news was coming through of a huge concentration camp called Auschwitz Birkenau which had just been liberated in Poland, and the finding stunned belief. It had been erected for the sole purpose of killing hundreds of thousands of Jewish people and disposing of their remains in a series of vast ovens and crematoria. This it turned out was part of Hitler's fiendish plan known as The Final Solution.

It was now obvious why the Jewish lads and the German POWs had been kept apart, though I doubt if any of them had been aware of this before our arrival in Taranto. News of any kind was always a 'semi-secret', even from us who had access to radio broadcasts. So for the time being I'm sure they were all in blissful ignorance of the horror.

We remained at anchor in Taranto harbour for a week disembarking, and then embarking another crowd. We were only allowed shore leave once, and the only clear memory I have of this was a visit to a servicemen's club, where the walls were decorated with drawings by some notable newspaper cartoonist. I was probably told his name at the time, but I've forgotten who he was.

Looking back I think it was probably about this time that I fell out with the bo's'n. And even though I'd been looking forward to staying on the *Alcantara*, after this I found it impossible due to the bad feeling between us. It all came about because he'd accused one of my watch of not securing a derrick properly. I knew this to be untrue because my watch hadn't used the derrick. The bo's'n soon found out the truth, but I had to ask him to let the seaman who'd been accused off the hook. It was then that I realised he was an unfair man and told him so. After that I don't think we spoke a civil word until I left the ship. One word from him, a simple 'sorry', would have saved all that acrimony.

We finally left Taranto and the voyage home was uneventful as far as enemy activity was concerned and it was common knowledge that our port of call in the UK was Liverpool. What I do remember vividly about that voyage home is the weather. After we'd cleared the Straits of Gibraltar we headed out into the Atlantic to avoid the Bay of Biscay and ran straight into the teeth of an Atlantic gale. All the deck crew spent a lousy, wet week double-checking everything that could move, and doubling up on lashings, etc. Most of us put in over a hundred hours of duty that week, and there was no extra money for overtime in those days. It was simply classed as, 'safety of the ship'. Eventually, as the storm abated, we turned in the direction of home, and those of us leaving the ship spent our spare time drying out damp clothing and packing for home.

At last we entered the Mersey on a cold, grey day in late February 1945, obviously delighted to be back in Blighty, though my feelings were tinged with regret, because if only the bo's'n had shown a little understanding I would have signed on again. However, he deliberately avoided me, so that was that. Fortunately regrets don't last long when you're twenty-one, so I put it behind me and looked forward to leave, and my next ship.

21

Leave in Barrow, and
Coals from Newcastle

It was now early March 1945 and after leaving the *Alcantara* I had eight days at home on leave. During my stay in Barrow this time I seemed to sense a feeling of resignation in most of the people I met. The allies were advancing in Europe, and the Russians were sweeping all before them in the east. Shipping losses were now as low as they'd been for a long time, but still the Germans were fighting as doggedly as ever for every inch of ground, and in the process inflicting heavy losses on our lads. I think that most people had long since given up hope of a swift victory. It seemed a long time since I'd heard anyone trot out the old optimistic claim, 'It'll all be over by Christmas'.

During that leave I saw a lot of lads who'd left home full of patriotism and bravado only to return now completely changed. One poor devil who I'd worked with as a fourteen year old milk boy – though he was about four years older than I was – was wheeled into a pub in an invalid chair paralysed from the waist down. He was with a crowd of family and friends and seemed to be putting on a brave show of acceptance. I shook his hand and muttered something glib, and probably silly, through embarrassment I think. But I knew at the time, and I think he also knew how bereft and forlorn his future would be. His wife was a bonny, caring person, and I've thought since how saddened and disillusioned she must have been to see all her hopes and aspirations for a full life shattered.

On another occasion, while walking along Barrow's main

shopping street, Dalton Road, I bumped into a lad I'd gone to school with. He was being guided by his mother, and was a complete shell-shocked wreck. My heart bled for him and his mother to think what a barren future lay ahead of them. He was dressed in the royal blue uniform of a wounded serviceman, and was home for a week from some hospital or other, where probably he was one of hundreds of other poor unfortunates, whose lives to all intents and purposes were over. The tragedy of it all was that apart from the victims themselves, all those who loved them had had an unbearable burden put upon them, consequently blighting their lives too.

Now sixty years on, after the tragedy in New York, I can see and hear all the armchair warriors again advocating full scale war, safe in the knowledge that *they* won't be affected no matter how many others are killed and mutilated. I think that if one tenth of the money spent on what has become known as the 'defence industry' was used to try and rectify the world's inequalities, terrorism would slowly die a death, and millions of people living in abject misery and squalor under despotic regimes would at last have that very necessary commodity that we all cherish, 'hope'.

Having got all that off my chest it's now back to 1945.

My leave being over I reported to the office of the shipping pool on the Strand in Barrow. Mr Garland, the crew officer, was waiting for me, and after his usual enquires about my health and the previous ship, I was told to return that afternoon to collect all my papers and a travel warrant. I, along with two other lads, was to join a ship called the SS *Brent Wood* at Blyth in Northumberland. She was owned and operated by a firm called the France Fenwick Steamship Company, which was solely concerned with the transport of coal.

I wasn't too impressed with this as I'd had my share of coal carrying vessels in the past. The simple reason being that on these ships the coal dust gets absolutely everywhere. Still, 'ours not to reason why', as they say. So the following day I set off with my two companions and arrived in Blyth about teatime.

We took a taxi to the docks and found our ship at the coal loading berth. She was typical of her class, being what was known as a, 'three island tramp', which meant that she had a raised forecastle, a raised bridge section in the middle and a raised stern (poop) section. In between these three 'islands' were four holds for cargo. She was similar to many hundreds built between the wars.

Our accommodation was forward in the fo'c'sle, and to say it was basic would be an overstatement. I've been told that prisoners in Her Majesty's jails have to have a certain cubic capacity of space to live in. The average tramp steamer gave each man about half as much, the only guarantee being that he'd at least have a bunk.

As I said, we'd arrived about teatime, and as we were hungry after our long journey we made our way amidships to see if there was any food on the go. We were unlucky, everything was closed and not a sign of anything to eat in the galley. However, I was familiar with the layout of the midships accommodation on that type of ship, so I soon found the chief steward's cabin. When we did manage to get him to open his cabin door he started to bluster about mealtimes etc. By this time the three of us were getting a bit fed up, so the 'fireman' among us who hadn't spoken more than a dozen words since leaving Barrow, surprisingly pushed his face close to the steward's and said, "Look! if we don't get some food now, we're all going to get back on the train and return home. So make a decision one way or the other."

This took the bluster out of the chief steward altogether. It would seem that with the company having to drag three of its crew members from right across the country, there were obviously no locals available, so he daren't risk the anger of the skipper by losing us for the sake of a meal.

"Well, the cook has gone ashore," he said, "so I'll order you a taxi, and pay for a meal at a good hotel in Blyth." This was OK by us, and so after leaving our kit-bags in the fo'c'sle off we went and had a really good evening meal at what was at that time the best hotel in the town. Being taxied to and fro into the bargain, this was high living indeed.

The next day, however, we were inevitably brought back to earth with a bump. The bo's'n arrived with the news that after we'd eaten breakfast we were to move the ship to the coaling berth to take on our cargo.

After we'd moved the ship and opened up the four hatches ready for loading we all assembled in the captain's saloon to sign on, as until this was done we were not officially crew members. I signed, and that made me a rather reluctant AB on the SS

Brent Wood.

The next few days were taken up with moving the ship backwards and forwards under the coal chute. This was a gradual procedure in order to keep the ship trim whilst loading so she wouldn't sink down too much forward or aft under the weight. It was a really dirty job with everything soon covered under thick black dust. So it was a relief when we were at long last fully laden and able to batten down the hatches and prepare for sea; though where we were going was still a mystery.

With the loading now completed the deck crew, which comprised four able seamen, two ordinary seamen (juniors not yet qualified), and two deck boys, were split up into two groups and began hosing down. My group began on the 'monkey island', which is a platform above the bridge found on older ships. This is sometimes used for 'conning', or steering, the ship in any kind of emergency. On this particular day 'our' monkey island looked like the inside of a coal scuttle. Hosing down took quite a few hours, but eventually the SS *Brent Wood* began to resemble a ship again, and by then it was supper time.

I don't think any of us were quite prepared for the meal that was put in front of us. Merchant Navy cooks in general, although quite resourceful at providing hot meals under some horrendous conditions, could not by any stretch of the imagination be classed as Cordon Bleu. But this chap turned out to be a very welcome exception and supper that night was really enjoyable. At least this looked like being the one redeeming feature of the SS *Brent Wood*, because if the cook kept up this standard, shipboard life would be a lot more agreeable than I'd first thought.

The following day, with all battened down and ready for sea, the mate (chief officer) came forward to meet the deck crew, and I think formally introduce himself. He was with the bo's'n and seemed a decent sort of chap. He told us that our orders for sailing hadn't arrived yet, but he hazarded a guess at Antwerp in Belgium; which turned out to be correct.

Now that the allies had secured that port the dangerous business of clearing mines had begun, because Jerry, sensing defeat, had sewn mines indiscriminately in the Eastern and Western Schelde. Consequently mine-sweepers were now working flat out to clear them. No vital supplies could be brought in through Antwerp until the access to it was cleared. So to save

190

the mine-sweepers having to return to the UK to bunker up with coal every time, it would be our job to bring it in, and build up a stockpile for them to draw on.

We left Blyth fully laden and proceeded east-south-east. Five or six miles offshore we were joined by a mine-sweeping ex-trawler, which took up a position about four-hundred yards ahead. I guess the strategy would be that as we approached the Schelde he'd start actively sweeping for mines so as to clear a safe path for us. We all sincerely hoped he'd be successful!

So we settled down to the normal business of sailing a tramp steamer. On the first day there was a bitterly cold wind blowing from the east, and the old ship, heavily laden as she was, was wallowing like a pregnant cow. There were only enough crew to run two watches; four hours on and four off. The two watches swapped over at 4pm each day at what are known as the Dog Watches (two short watches 4–6pm and 6–8pm). This meant that the watch due on at 4pm only did two hours and the watch due on at 6pm also only did two hours. A complicated system, but quite effective.

On each normal four hour watch myself and the other able seaman on my watch did two hours at the wheel, and two hours lookout duty on the fo'c'sle head. As we also had two ordinary seamen on each watch they were able to relieve us both for a fifteen minute break now and then, which was always most welcome.

I felt sorry for the lads on the mine-sweeper out in front, because every time she plunged into the sea she was covered in spray, and I can't imagine that on board what pre-war had been a deep sea trawler they'd have many facilities for drying clothes. To make matters worse the seasoned fishermen who normally manned these old trawlers had been replaced by the present crew. All of whom were lads called up for war-service, and had probably never even seen a trawler before. Fortunately, their skippers were invariably ex-seagoing types and widely experienced.

On the afternoon of the third day our mine-sweeper put up a string of flags, which when deciphered from our code book told us that we were to be extra vigilant, because it appeared that a rogue U-boat had been discovered hiding among the Frisian Islands. He'd probably be captained by some diehard who knew the war was lost, but wanted to wreak some last ditch damage.

However, extra lookouts were impossible as we hadn't the men to do it. What crew we had were scarcely enough to run the ship as it was. As the Yanks would say, 'We'd have to put our faith in the Lord,' although this didn't seem to have done much good up to now.

We knew we were approaching the Schelde, which is the waterway leading into Antwerp, when the mine-sweeper hoisted another flag signal to say they were about to start sweeping for mines ahead of us in order to give us a clear channel. Once again we could only hope that they'd be a hundred per cent successful. Fortunately they were.

Once inside the Schelde and past Flushing on the Dutch side of the estuary it didn't take long to reach Antwerp harbour, and by dusk that day we were safely tied up at the discharging berth in Siberia Dock with our vital supply of coal.

Our first job was to open up all the hatches so as to be ready for offloading the next day. With all the huge cranes we could see along the dockside, we thought that this would be a straight-forward job and they'd soon have us unloaded. But to our disappointment we soon discovered that Jerry had sabotaged them all, which meant we'd have to use the ship's own derricks in what would obviously be a slow drawn out procedure.

The Belgian dockers worked hard loading the coal into tubs, which we then swung ashore to be emptied into trucks for delivery to the stockpile. It was a weary and laborious job, but there was no alternative.

One thing I particularly remember from that occasion was how our ship's cook, who as I've said earlier was a revelation in the standard of his cooking, went up to the mate's quarters after breakfast on that first day. This in itself was a most unusual event, but it turned out that he'd sought, and got, permission to make a huge pan of broth to distribute to the Belgian stevedores. They were sent to the galley in twos, and I've never seen such appreciation of a kindly deed before.

The cook also gave each one of them half a loaf of bread, and considering he had to hand bake all our bread this was an especially decent gesture. He told me later that none of them had touched the bread, but had wrapped it up carefully, so it was obvious to him that it would be going home to their families.

These people must have had an appalling existence on starvation rations under German occupation.

The discharge of our cargo took almost a fortnight to complete, and our chief officer hazarded the opinion that the Belgian dockers had deliberately taken their time in order to prolong their daily soup ration. If so, good luck to them!

Finally the last tub of coal was swung ashore and we battened down the hatches. Then once again we hosed down the ship before setting sail. Halfway down the Schelde our old friend the mine-sweeper joined us to sweep a channel out into the North Sea. Our orders were to return to Blyth for another cargo of coal and return once more to Antwerp. We were all rather pleased about this, as we'd been given no shore leave in Belgium, so were looking forward to a night out in Blyth and a few pints of good Geordie beer.

We landed back in Blyth without incident and moored at the coal loading berth once more, though not looking forward to all the muck and dust that loading coal entailed. After drawing some money from the skipper, off we went to sample Blyth's best bitter, followed by a good old fish and chip supper eaten from newspaper. Then four hours later, feeling rather the worse for wear, we all staggered back aboard.

Our last night in Blyth was spent in the vaults of a nearby pub, where we'd become friendly with some of the locals. I learned from them that just prior to the war there'd been a local branch of the Communist Party, which despite being small in numbers had been successful in preventing thousands-odd tons of scrap metal from being shipped to Japan by our great industrial 'patriots'. As usual they were vilified at the time by the powers that be. Nevertheless they banned anyone locally from handling the scrap, and called on their friends on the railway not to move it elsewhere. Lo and behold, when war was declared some months later they were suddenly regarded as far-seeing heroes who'd saved valuable steel for the war effort.

Some days later, around the first week in April 1945, we were fully loaded again, so battened down the hatches, hosed and cleaned the ship and set sail for Antwerp. On this voyage it was assumed that the North Sea was now safe, and we were to have no escort. If I remember correctly, the weather was chilly but mild, at least there was no wind . . . how strange when you think

j

that in the days of our predecessors 'wind' was the vital factor in driving their ships along, while now in the age of mechanical power it was nothing but a curse.

So we settled down once more to the monotonous routine of four hours on and four hours off, with the only consolation being that it wasn't a very long trip to Antwerp. The other able seaman and I, together with the two ordinary seamen who formed our watch, took over the first dog watch at 4pm. At about 5pm I was at the wheel, with the others on lookout and stand-by, when approximately forty miles from the Schelde Estuary the first deafening explosion hit us. At first it was hard to grasp what had happened, because for the past few months we'd all been lulled into a false sense of security. But within three or four minutes there was a second huge explosion and my first thoughts were that we'd been torpedoed twice. Fortunately I was wrong.

After the initial shock it suddenly dawned on me that the wheel in my hands had been rendered useless, and that the ship's engines had stopped. We had already begun to list to port and were down at the stern. The chief officer had rushed aft to assess the situation, and the skipper was in the process of sending out an SOS signal. As he was doing so my watch-mate, who'd been on lookout in the bow, arrived on the bridge to say that prior to the explosions he'd spotted some semi-submerged objects just off the port bow. However, he'd had no time to report them for the simple reason that he'd had no means of communication with the bridge, and in any event the mines had been too close and had detonated the moment they touched.

My watch's action station in the event of such a catastrophe was at the starboard lifeboat, where we were to prepare it for lowering ready to evacuate the ship. On this occasion, however, this was impossible due to the ship's list to port. So, we joined the other watch in readying the port lifeboat for action.

In the meantime the chief officer had surveyed the damage and decided that in his opinion, bad as the damage was, he didn't think we would sink. Apparently the mines had struck just aft of number four hold, and the compartment that housed the steering gear was flooded. The stern-post for the rudder had also been badly damaged, and the chief believed that the propeller shaft had probably been bent as well.

Now that the initial shock had worn off, the mate and bo's'n decided that if possible we should all try to rig up some rope life-lines until assistance arrived. Unfortunately the rope and paint store was aft in a section above the damaged steering compartment. So hanging on to anything we could, three of us finally managed to reach the store only to find that the double explosion had twisted the steel door and jammed it shut. We struggled with it for a while but in the end had to give up and drag ourselves back amidships.

To add to the discomfort it had begun to pour with rain and dusk was settling in. The North Sea seemed a really cold and inhospitable place on that day. Two of the able seamen and the cook were down in the galley trying to salvage at least some of what would have been our supper. The galley fires which were coal fed had gone out, and it was too risky to try and relight them. Luckily there was plenty of cold meat and bread to keep us going so it was simply a matter of waiting for an answer to our distress signal. For the time being the skipper had decided not to abandon ship, because although badly listing and down at the stern we still seemed to be buoyant.

Just before dark set in, as we were still wallowing helplessly, two Royal Navy torpedo boats approached at high speed travelling north. As they neared and saw our predicament they slowed and circled us. Then one came alongside and asked through a loudhailer if we needed any immediate help. But there was nothing they could do, because what we really needed were tugs to tow us somewhere where we could offload and survey the damage. So away they went at breakneck speed. We learned later that they were out searching for a new type of U-boat which was operating some fifty miles to the north, in the area of the Firth of Forth.

We now put four men on lookout in order to cover all directions. The ship's steward gave blankets to those on watch, while the skipper sent the rest below to try and get some sleep. And even though it was like lying on the side of a hill at least we were sheltered and by now dry.

As dawn broke the following day it was all hands on deck to see if there was any activity on the horizon. After what seemed like weeks, but in reality was about eight hours we spotted a ship of some sort approaching from the west. This was a bit of a mystery, since because of our position we'd expected our SOS to be answered from the Antwerp direction. The vessel turned out to be a tug from Hull, and it turned out that our original request for assistance had not been acted upon due to some foul up in communications. Thankfully the skipper of one of the torpedo boats had reported our position on returning from patrol, and here was the result.

The tug eventually drew alongside and its captain had a word with our skipper. Between them it was decided that we should be taken in tow, though where to was a different proposition. They'd contacted the authorities in Antwerp and though the reasoning behind their reply was sensible, it was no help to us. They'd decided that unless someone higher up made an order, they dare not risk us sinking in the entrance to the Schelde and blocking what was their main supply route.

However, while this was being sorted out the tug began the tow. It soon became obvious that we would need another tug on our stern, because with our rudder jammed over to starboard our ship was dragging to port and putting too much strain on the tug ahead. The dead propeller wasn't helping either.

This controlled towing at two or three knots went on until night fell, and by this time we were all beginning to feel the strain and tempers were fraying. Another long night followed during which we had to keep watch in twos on the fo'c'sle head, ready to slip the tow wire in any emergency. This would have been a lousy job even if the ship had been on an even keel, but the fact that it was listing more than fifteen degrees to port made it so much more trying.

However, daybreak brought good news. Another tug was on its way, and they'd decided that our cargo was so urgently needed in Antwerp that we were to be towed into Siberia Dock after all. The tug duly arrived and took a wire rope from our stern bollards, and so we continued our ill-fated journey which had begun so hopefully a few days earlier.

To add to our problems the poor cook was now running out of food, for the simple reason that the galley fires couldn't be lit. So during the tow, which lasted forty-eight hours, we were rationed to two slices of corned beef and two biscuits. To make matters worse and pile on the misery, my watch-mate and I had developed shivering colds and it was all we could do to keep awake during our watches over the tow-wires.

However, at long last we reached the coaling wharf in Antwerp and were manoeuvred alongside by our tugs. A welcome bit of good news that greeted us this time was that one of the dockside cranes had been repaired, so at least offloading the coal wouldn't be quite so long and drawn out. Nevertheless, the job of taking off the hatch covers was daunting enough. I personally felt so weak and wretched due to the fever that I seemed to be working in a trance. Once we'd got the hatch covers off it became obvious why we'd got such a severe list to port. The coal had shifted to that side due to the two explosions.

Once the ship had been readied for the dock workers, the skipper and chief officer broke another piece of good news. It seemed we were to be treated as 'survivors' and taken away for medical treatment, rest and we hoped some decent hot food.

Shortly afterwards two canvas-topped army trucks arrived and the whole crew, except for the officers, were helped into them. The journey took almost an hour, and I think we must have dozed all the way as I don't remember much of it. We eventually arrived at a large chateau type of house in a place called Hemiksen, which I think was on the Albert Canal on the outskirts of Antwerp.

During the German occupation its inhabitants had been turned out, and the Germans used it as a kind of country club for those of high rank. Now, however, it was a headquarters for the British Army Medical Corps, and you can believe me when I say they were kindness itself.

By this time we were all ravenous with hunger, and my watch-mate and myself were also flushed and sweating with fever. In the dining hall I think I managed some soup, but immediately became nauseous and brought it all back up. A young army doctor was brought and after the usual temperature checks etc., we were both taken to a kind of dormitory, and I've never been so glad to get into bed and rest in my life.

I think my mate was worse than I was because I could hear him semi-consciously moaning all night. Although two days later the orderly who'd been detailed to keep an eye on us told me that it was me who was moaning and not him.

We were there for a week and just as I was beginning to enjoy my convalescence we were told to get ready to leave, because we were either going back to the ship where we'd left all our belongings, such as they were, or being shipped home if it was found impossible to sail or tow her back to the UK. By this time our whole crew were beginning to feel like human beings again, and like me were enjoying the routine of three decent meals a day and plenty of rest.

During our stay at the medical centre, news had been coming in all the time of concentration camps being discovered, and of the unspeakable conditions prevailing in them. I've always maintained, then and now, that the general public in Germany were either oblivious of what was going on – 'none so blind as those who will not see' – or else they knew and simply didn't care. Who would have guessed then, that in spite of all the evil the Germans had done, within a few short years they would be allowed to become the economic powerhouse of Europe. Encouraged obviously in this by those elements opposed to the growing power of the Soviet Union.

On the evening of our last day we were taken to a small provincial cinema nearby which was packed with British servicemen, but I don't know where it was. I do remember that the film was one of Abbot & Costello's. The pictures that had us on the edge of our seats though, were what we saw on the Movietone News which was also showing. It was full of images of the victims of the Nazi's 'Final Solution', who were being liberated from various death camps. We could hardly believe it possible that human beings could inflict such vile, appalling misery on others.

It should be remembered, of course, that in those days there was no such thing as television. And that the only place where visual news could be seen was at the cinema through such news films as shown by Movietone News, Pathé News and an American film company called The March of Time. These all showed films of the recent, or fairly recent, big news events of the time in an encapsulated, digest form. Nowadays we just turn on the TV for this.

After our visit to the cinema we were taken back to the château to spend our last night, still uncertain about the plans for our tomorrow.

Next day the trucks turned up to return us to the ship. We'd all very much appreciated our short break, and gave our thanks and good-byes gratefully to the people who'd looked after us so well.

When we eventually arrived back in the harbour, we found that the ship had been moved to another part of the dock after having had its cargo of coal offloaded. What a tribute it was to the honesty of the Belgian dockers to find that all our belongings were just as we had left them.

The chief officer then turned up and informed us that for the time being the ship was to remain in Antwerp. I think the damage was so extensive that she was only fit for scrap. Anyway, once we'd collected our gear we were taken by lorry to a kind of transit camp down the Schelde about an hour and a half's drive from Antwerp. We were housed in Nissen type huts, and though it was basic it was more comfortable than some ships I'd sailed in.

A somewhat larger hut served as a mess-room, and in the evenings was utilised as a social centre. Believe me, the whole war was fought over and over again in theory during our evenings in that hut. We were a good cross section of all the services, and there was no doubt that the future of Great Britain was the one topic that united us all. One thing that was accepted unanimously was that even though old 'Winnie', as Churchill was affectionately known, had been an exceptionally good war leader with great personnel and oratorial skills, these were not going to be enough to give us the kind of Britain that we'd fought for and deserved. In any case his pre-war, outright antagonism to the aspirations of the working class population were too well documented to be ignored. None of the blokes I talked to wanted to go back to the 'dole queue mentality' of the inter-war years, and were convinced that Churchill was definitely not the man who could be trusted to make great changes in this. I always remember the words of the film star Edward G. Robinson when he was asked who he thought was the greatest actor he'd ever seen, and he replied emphatically, "Winston Churchill."

However, we'd have to wait and see what would happen when the war was over and the wartime coalition government came to an end.

We stayed in the transit camp for almost a week, with each day some of us being chosen for return to the United Kingdom. At last my turn came, and together with three of my shipmates I was embarked on a converted trawler for the North Sea crossing.

After a quiet, uneventful trip we landed back in Hull on the 7th May 1945, the day before VE-Day (Victory in Europe Day). And to quote an old jazz expression, 'The Joint Was Jumpin' '.

We were met at the docks by an agent of France Fenwick, the shipping company that we'd sailed with. He had with him all our papers, discharge books and travel vouchers, plus an advance on wages owing – the rest to be forwarded to our home port shipping offices later.

Once all the formalities were over none of us wasted any time in heading for the railway station, eager to get home and share in the festivities amongst family and friends.

The train pulled into Barrow Station at six o'clock in the morning, and it felt wonderful to be back. I had to walk from the station to Hindpool, and even at that time in the morning there were plenty of people about and for once it seemed that the traditional British reserve had been forgotten. Everyone was aware that the war was at an end, or at least the European war was, and as I walked home through the streets a few intrepid women and older men were already busy erecting trestle tables for the parties that were to come later.

As I passed by with my kit-bag on my shoulder many of them shouted "Good Luck lad! It's all over now." I couldn't have answered them as I had a lump in my throat, both from realising that I'd actually survived the war, and knowing how genuine and sincere people like these were when called upon to unite against adversity. They were worth a lot better life than the one they'd endured before the war, and hopefully they'd get it.

My mother was absolutely delighted to see me, of course, but had been hoping to see *all* her children home at this time. Unfortunately, however, Jim was still out in Ceylon and would be for some time, and Bill, who was now married, would be staying at his home in London when he was demobbed.

I was now officially on leave, but would still have to sign on at the pool office in the Strand on the following day to see if there were any changes yet in my status now that the war was over. In the meantime I was determined to join in the celebrations that were going on all over town. Street parties were rollicking on through the night and there was no shortage of beer. I think that a lot of pubs simply ignored closing times and stayed open, and the constabulary turned a blind eye. It was dawn on the 9th May when we, that is myself and some old shipmates who were also home, drank our last toast to absent friends and groggily staggered home.

Later that day, still feeling very fragile, I made my way to the pool office on the Strand to see the pool officer, Mr Garland. I wanted to know if anything had changed, but it appeared that nothing had. He'd received notification from the Ministry of Transport that the emergency powers act was still in force, and that we were still obliged to register for service on ships as we'd done before. I was quite pleased at this news as I fully intended to carry on as a seaman, at least for now. I felt it would be quite a novelty to climb into a ship's bunk secure in the knowledge that there was no U-boat lurking out in the depths waiting to fire a torpedo at us.

So there, for what they are worth, are my recollections of those fifteen crucial years in my early life which stretched from the misery and deprivation of the 1930s to the end of the war in May 1945.

I've often thought that if war can ever be justified, 'Our War', as I call it, was the only one that *had* to be fought. My only wish at the time it ended was that it hadn't all been in vain. That something better than the diabolical pre-war conditions would surely emerge as a monument to all those who sadly had not lived to see the results of their supreme sacrifice.

22

My Post-War Seafaring –
A Brief Summary

Although the war in Europe was over after almost six terrible years – or at least the 'shooting' war was – the protagonists were now left with the massive problem of rehabilitating the untold millions of displaced people who were scattered all over Europe. And also, of course, bringing to justice all those whose crimes against humanity had caused all this unimaginable misery, and carnage with a death toll not then fully known, but certain to run into many millions. On top of all this the war was definitely not over for all those tragic victims still searching for loved ones, friends and family, who in all probability they'd never see again. Added to all this anguish was the daily struggle for survival they faced on a continent where food was in very short supply, and even basic shelter for many was virtually non-existent.

As far as I was concerned my first ship after the war's end was a Baron boat. These were owned by the Hogarths Shipping Company, trading from Ardrossan in Western Scotland. They were usually engaged in carrying bulk cargoes such as iron ore and coal. The nomenclature of their ships was always '*Baron . . .* something or other'. To the crews they were also known, justifiably, as 'Hungry Hogarths'. I eventually sailed on a few of them, and the food was invariably poor in both quantity and quality. An old joke about them concerned one old sailor addressing another who'd got a thin, drawn-in face and asking him: "Are you whistling or have you just done a trip on one of Hogarths' ships?"

However, I joined my first Baron boat, the *Baron Ruthven*, at Workington in Cumberland a few weeks after the war ended, where she had just discharged a cargo of Spanish wolfram (tungsten) ore. We took her light ship north and through the Pentland Firth to Methil in Fife Scotland. Here without much delay we loaded coal for Lubeck in Germany. Once again this was to fuel mine-sweepers who were sweeping the Baltic Sea where, as elsewhere, Jerry had sewn mines indiscriminately. If they ever *had* marked the positions of these mines on charts, then they'd destroyed the charts out of sheer badness.

We entered the mouth of the Elbe River and then passed through the Kiel Canal into the Baltic Sea, and on to Lubeck. Lubeck was a fine old city, and the armed forces there had set up a club, the White Crusader Club, for all service personnel. We were made more than welcome and spent some happy hours there.

It was in Lubeck on the outskirts of the city that I saw at first hand, in Displaced Persons' Camps, the full terrible effects that the war had had on those 'pressed' into the service of the Third Reich. The different nationalities in these camps were too many to guess at. They even included Moroccan soldiers from the Blue Brigade that the Spanish dictator Franco had sent to the Russian front to assist his friend Adolf Hitler. All of these people seemed desperate to find someone with the authority to enable them to return home.

It must be realised, however, that at that time all transport, but particularly the railways, was in a worse state than in Britain at the moment. Though in our present rail shambles in Britain we can't fall back on the excuse of intensive air bombardment, which the continentals could in those days.

To make matters worse the German currency was useless, so the British authorities had introduced a type of emergency currency to bridge the gap. I can't remember its name, but I think it was referred to as 'Occupation Money' or 'Scrip'. However, the real bargaining was being done using cigarettes, coffee, etc., which at that time were priceless.

Once our cargo had been discharged we set sail back for the UK but were held up at the Baltic end of the Kiel Canal due to some accident or other. Whilst waiting we decided to take a trip ashore into Kiel itself that evening. This turned out to be a bad mistake as we discovered that there were gangs of what were nicknamed 'Werewolves' roaming the streets, intent on doing as much harm as possible to any allied servicemen they came across. Although the members of these gangs were only teenagers, they were armed with an assortment of vicious-looking clubs and chains, and more than one soldier received a terrible beating from them. Luckily for us there were eight or nine in our group. Nevertheless we made our way back aboard as quickly as possible; discretion being the better part of valour.

Eventually our ship arrived back in Newcastle where, having had enough of Hogarth cuisine, I paid off. After such a short trip it would have been a waste of time and money to go back to Barrow, and fortunately I heard about a ship belonging to an old company I'd sailed with before who were looking for a deck crew. This was the *Kirkwood* belonging to the France Fenwick shipping company who operated from Newcastle, so I managed to sign on with them and did another short trip, this time to Hamburg itself.

This visit to Hamburg was a staggering eye-opener for me. I'd seen bomb damage in many parts of the UK including London, Glasgow, Liverpool etc., but none of these prepared me for the complete and utter devastation of this once beautiful 'Hanseatic League' city. It was nothing but rubble as far as the eye could see. I learned that the loss of life had been horrific, and that in one night alone there'd been forty-thousand deaths when the whole city went up like a torch in a fire-storm which literally sucked all the oxygen from people's lungs.

This proved to me more than ever what I said earlier in these memoirs, that the whole campaign of indiscriminate destruction carried out by both the German and the Allied Air Forces may have killed vast numbers of innocent civilians, but did not shorten the war by a single day. This is because instead of sapping the morale of the civilian populations thus attacked it actually had the opposite effect of stiffening their resistance. I have argued this with different people many times, and believe my theory was finally vindicated during the war in Vietnam. The Americans dropped more high explosives there than had been used by both sides in the Second World War. They also dropped thousands of tons of one of the most deadly biological weapons known. This was called Agent Orange and was designed to destroy vast areas of the jungle in which the Vietnamese enemy forces were operating. It certainly destroyed the jungles, but not the morale of the Vietnamese enemy. They simply created living quarters and hospitals underground and carried on fighting. The end result being an ignominious defeat for the richest, most powerful nation on Earth, who had to scuttle away with their tails between their legs. Agent Orange unfortunately produced diabolical side effects, the consequences of which are still being seen even today, thirty years later, in the hundreds of deformed Vietnamese children that were born.

This, by the way, is the same America that demanded to inspect Iraq's potential for producing biological and chemical weapons of mass destruction . . . I believe this is called 'double standards'.

However, I think I'd better get off my soap box again.

When we arrived back in the UK from Hamburg and sailed up the River Tyne I decided that I'd had my fill of the SS *Kirkwood*, so was paid off and made my way home. After only three or four days in Barrow I was sent up to the port of Silloth near Carlisle on the Solway Firth to join a coaster called the *Alacrity*. She was only about three-hundred tons displacement and spent her life sailing back and forth across the Irish sea to many different places in Ireland. I sailed aboard her for about six months, and quite enjoyed visiting most of the ports in both Northern and Southern Ireland.

The *Alacrity*'s skipper was quite a character. He was from Rush in what was then known as The Irish Free State. His name was Tom Rooney, so I immediately nicknamed him Mickey after the American film star. He always referred to me as 'Joe Stallion' (Stalin) because of my, to him, terrible views on socialism. In spite of this we always got on well, and I respected him not least because he was a damned fine seaman.

After I left the *Alacrity* I was getting a bit fed up with the endless toing and froing and applied for permission to try shore life for a while. I was reminded that even though the war was over I was still beholden to the Emergency Powers Act. Even so, I was granted twelve months leave of absence, without pay, and still being required to report once a month to the shipping office in Barrow.

I tried two or three different jobs during this time ashore. I also got married, which ended in failure and acrimony, leaving me a sadder and, I wish I could say, a wiser man.

After all this trauma I'd had enough of life ashore, so I got in touch with my union rep; who advised me to get back to sea as soon as I could find a ship. This turned out to be sound advice and in April 1947 I was sent to Southampton to join the magnificent old liner the *Aquitania*, a four-funnelled beauty that I'd seen many times during the war, never once thinking that one day I would sail in her.

Once I'd settled down on board the ship I spent all my off-watch time getting to know her and marvelling at the utter luxury she must have offered her passengers in her heyday.

I'd always heard that the crew's food on Cunard ships was good, and the *Aquitania* proved this beyond doubt.

When I joined her she was engaged in returning personnel to Canada and the United States as their tours of duty in occupied Europe came to an end. On our return voyages we would bring back hundreds of disillusioned GI brides, who'd married US servicemen in Great Britain only to come up against hard reality on arrival in the States. For a lot of these women their marriages had simply collapsed, and they had no alternative but to return home.

At the end of September 1947 the Cunard Company decided that it was now no longer economical to continue running the old *Aquitania* and she would be scrapped. All except a skeleton crew were paid off much to my regret as I, for one, was very sorry to see her go.

A week after having to leave the *Aquitania* so sadly, I joined a ship in Barrow Docks bound for Canada to pick up a cargo of timber. There was nothing distinguished about her, she was just a typical British tramp steamer; though I must admit the accommodation, which was still aft, was better than in most ships of this type.

The ship's name had the prefix *Avis*, and it was said that the owners of the ship were ex-RAF officers, and that this was their first ship. Whether this was true I don't know, but over the years I did see other ships with this prefix. And eventually the world-wide car rental firm of Avis appeared, and I've often wondered if there was a connection.

After a period on her I joined a Standard oil tanker and it was quite an experience. After several weeks at sea we docked at

Abadan in Iran. Abadan lay at the confluence of the two rivers Tigris and Euphrates. This area was called the Shatt Al Arab, or Waters of Arabia. At that time there was a great deal of national unrest in the area, so we weren't allowed to go ashore. It seemed that the Iranians, quite reasonably in my opinion, wanted more benefit from the oil that we and the Americans were taking from the vast oil fields all around the Persian Gulf.

As it turned out, being confined to the ship was academic as we weren't there long enough to go ashore. I think it only took about two days to fill up the ship, before, loaded to the tank tops, we were on our way home to the UK. I remember deciding at that time, that tankers were definitely not my kind of ship at all.

And so for the next few years I went from one ship to another almost automatically. I did trips to Spain, Italy and most of the ports in the Mediterranean, North Africa, West Africa, East Africa, the Americas North and South, but slowly I was beginning to lose interest; the gilt was wearing off the gingerbread.

I'd also noticed that the attitude of ship owners had changed. Now that the Ministry of War Transport was being wound down, things were beginning to revert to their peacetime status. The owners now had to pay their own bills, and the consequence was an all-out economy drive. I'll give the reader three guesses as to whom these economies were directed at. Yes, you're right, it was the crews as usual. The first noticeable thing to suffer was the food, which deteriorated in both quality and quantity as costs were cut to the bone – obviously to keep profit margins as high as possible.

The reader may have begun to wonder why I keep making reference to the food on ships, so a little explanation may help. Before the war, and until I came ashore in the nineteen-fifties there was no provision on any ship I sailed on for any kind of entertainment. There were no TVs or portable radio sets in those days, so when at sea it was simply a case of 'watch on' and 'watch off'. On most ships there was a crew's mess-room where, weather permitting, a kind of social life existed, though a game of cards or a good book to read was about the limit of this. Once at sea there was also, crucially, no means of obtaining any kind of food or refreshment other than that served up at the set mealtimes. Consequently, if the food in general was plentiful and decently cooked it made all the difference to the quality of life on what were sometimes very long voyages. In other words the 'grub' situation could make all the difference between a happy ship and a disgruntled one. Hence my constant emphasis on it.

Towards the end of 1949 I arrived at Workington in what was then Cumberland (now Cumbria) on board the *Empire Consistence* with a cargo of iron ore from Spain. It took about a week to unload this, and as I'd only signed on for the one trip, I had the choice of either re-signing for another trip or leaving. I didn't really fancy Spain again, or the iron ore trade, so I was somewhat undecided in the matter. However, I learned that there was another ship in the dock at that time which was looking for a crew. The ship was the *Cydonia*, and I heard on the grapevine that she was sailing down to Cardiff to pick up a cargo of Welsh coal for the Far East, and that once out there she would then carry on tramping from port to port before returning home. This sounded a much more attractive prospect than bucketing across the Bay of Biscay to Spain in mid-winter. In fact there was no contest, so I signed off the *Empire Consistence*, and signed on the *Cydonia*. As it turned out, however, this was not one of my best decisions.

We duly sailed for Cardiff when at about three o'clock on the afternoon of October 21st we struck a mine and the ship immediately began to founder. We were about halfway across Cardigan Bay, and it was blowing a force seven to eight gale with squally rain.

At the moment of the explosion I was down in one of the cargo holds with two ordinary seamen, cleaning it out ready for our next cargo. One of them remained calm, but the other one became hysterical and we had to virtually carry him up the ladder to the deck in what was a race against time. We had no idea what we'd find on deck, or how long we had before the ship sank – or even worse from our point of view, turned over before we'd got a chance to get a lifeboat away.

In the event we managed to lower a boat and get everyone off the stricken vessel in time. The chief mate put me at the stern with a long steering oar, but all I could do was keep the boats bow facing into the considerable wind. To add to the difficulties we had two or three women in the lifeboat, who as can be imagined were petrified with fear. The seas, which from the deck had looked rough enough, were a hundred times worse from a small lifeboat.

The women, who were the wives of the first officer and two of the engineers, had been looking forward to a few days with their husbands only to find themselves caught up in this terrible situation. As well as being frightened to death they were also violently sick.

As darkness fell things began to look ominous. The wind was worsening and we were bouncing from one wave to another, covered in spray, all thoroughly wet through and miserable. And then the most welcome sight we could have wished for came in the shape of a Dutch coaster. She turned out to be the *Mary Rose*, who had answered our mayday calls and had been searching for us for some hours in the gloom. With expert seamanship their skipper brought us up to his lee side and it didn't take long to get us all safely on board.

We were landed at Swansea the following day where we were all issued with warm clothing and spent a few days in the Seamans' Home. Fortunately, being young, we all recovered quickly and were soon back to normal.

I was soon on my way home to Barrow again where I found our story of peacetime shipwreck to be headline news in the local newspapers.

As I've explained earlier in these memoirs, if a seaman was shipwrecked or torpedoed during the war years he was entitled to the princely sum of £13.16/- to replace all his lost clothing, etc. We thought that this still applied and that we would receive this sum, but discovered that due to the fact that the war had been over for four years this largesse had been withdrawn by the authorities. Apparently no one had thought that the thousands of mines sewed both by us and the Germans would be likely to come popping to the surface once their moorings had rusted away.

Some months later though, I did receive an itemised bill explaining that I had after all been awarded my £13.16/- less about £9 for the clothing supplied in Swansea, which we'd foolishly thought was free. What a grateful nation we have. I never did find out who my generous benefactors were or I'd have written to thank then for their kindness – I don't think!

Following the loss of the *Cydonia* I was sent to join a small experimental tanker in the docks at Barrow. It was called the *Spabeck* and was the parent ship for a new, revolutionary type of submarine. This small experimental sub was called the Meteorite and used hydrogen peroxide as its fuel – which was, in fact, rocket fuel. The tanker *Spabeck* had a special pressurised tank in its hold to carry this liquid, which must have been pretty dangerous stuff because there were shower heads set up on deck where one could go to get washed off if any of it splashed onto you.

I believe that towards the end of the war Jerry had been experimenting with this process, and the British had brought these scientists (and families) over to Barrow and installed them secretly in a large house in Abbey Road to continue their research. The submarine was apparently expected to be capable of speeds in excess of twenty knots under water, which would have enabled it to torpedo its victims and escape unharmed by sheer speed.

We only did one trial in the Irish Sea and the sub did all that was claimed for it. However, when it surfaced the underwater pressure had literally bent the conning tower and the hatch had to be forced open.

Shortly after this I left the *Spabeck*. I wasn't suited to life as a boffin, or a boffin's assistant. In any case I believe that due to the advance in nuclear propulsion systems the whole project was eventually dropped.

My seagoing career was then followed on numerous ships and various voyages to a great variety of destinations. These included Germany, France and most of the Mediterranean ports; Atlantic crossings to most of the American and Canadian seaports. Finally I did an iron ore run to North Africa on a ship which carried a huge deck cargo of esparto grass for good measure.

It was after this trip that I decided to apply for permission to break my contract and try life ashore. I'd sailed on over forty different ships, and quite frankly it was starting to become the same old procedure over and over. Another factor in my decision was the intake of new seamen starting to arrive on the scene. To me they all seemed clueless, and with little desire to learn their trade at all. So, at the end of 1950 I paid off the *Baron Ruthven* and returned home to try life ashore again.

I stuck it out for about six weeks, during which time I tried three or four different jobs, and could settle in none of them. It was then that I bumped into an old shipmate who told me he was going to join a ship in Swansea, and that there was room for one more able seaman. After thinking it over I decided to join him for just one more trip. Looking back I should have run a mile in the opposite direction.

When we got to Swansea the following day the ship turned out to be the *Sea Fisher*; the only one of the Fisher fleet to sail deep sea. We sailed on the same tide bound for Hamburg in Germany. The ship was engaged in transporting machinery etc., to Brest in France and other destinations. I quickly found that I didn't like the ship, her captain or any of her officers, on top of this the food was terrible. I couldn't have been more glad when we returned to the UK and I paid off.

Despite the above experience I joined another ship belonging to Harrisons of London. But after one trip to Rotterdam I finally realised that I'd definitely had enough. My last short spell ashore had made me realise how much I missed being able to have a social life; which is impossible at sea.

That was the end of my seagoing career. I'd enjoyed it immensely and had no regrets, having been privileged to actually see a world I could only ever have imagined had I not taken the path that I did.